You Can't *Say* That in Canada!

Also Available from Margaret Wente

An Accidental Canadian

MARGARET WENTE

You Can't *Say* That in Canada!

HarperCollins*Publishers*Ltd

You Can't Say That in Canada!
© 2009 by Margaret Wente.
All rights reserved.

Published by HarperCollins Publishers Ltd

Selections from the book have previously appeared in *The Globe and Mail*.

First Edition

HarperCollins books may be purchased for educational, business,
or sales promotional use through our Special Markets Department.

HarperCollins Publishers Ltd
2 Bloor Street East, 20th floor
Toronto, Ontario, Canada
M4W 1A8

www.harpercollins.ca

Library and Archives Canada Cataloguing in Publication

Wente, Margaret, 1950–
You can't say that in Canada: Canada's most influential columnist
reflects on life, politics and the pursuit of happiness / Margaret Wente.

ISBN 978-1-55468-468-7

1. Wente, Margaret, 1950–.
2. Journalists—Canada—Biography.
3. Women journalists—Canada–Biography.
I. Title.

PN4913.W46A3 2009   070.92   C2009-903131-0

RRD 9 8 7 6 5 4 3 2

Text design by Sharon Kish

For my sister Carrie

Contents

Why I Write

I've always been a bit of a contrarian. When everyone else was going one way, I wondered what it might be like to go the other. As a kid, I was lured by the forbidden. One day in Grade Three I decided to sit in the back of the bus—the boys' section, where no girls were allowed—just to see what might happen. Even then, I liked stirring things up. I'm glad to say I escaped with only insults.

I was a little feminist before my time, but by the time feminism came into full bloom I began to have my doubts about that, too. Was the patriarchy really all that bad? Was it really fair to pin the blame on men for all that ailed us? As the years went by, I came to see that the majority opinion wasn't *always* wrong—although that notion as an intellectual proposition was not a bad place to start.

One of my early heroes was George Orwell, the British journalist who tackled all manner of foolishness, self-deceit and cant. When the fashionable elites were embracing Stalin's Russia, he wrote *Animal Farm*. "To see what is before one's nose needs a constant struggle," he once wrote. Those are words I try to live by.

I used to think the trajectory of my working life was completely accidental. I never had a five-year plan, and I certainly never thought I'd wind up with my very own soapbox at *The Globe and Mail*. When I was young, women didn't do things like that. For many years I worked behind the scenes at the paper, making other people shine. I always liked to be provocative, of course. One of my triumphs as editor of *Report on Business Magazine* was persuading Harry Rosen, the famous men's clothier, to pose for a photo that showed him completely *un*clothed, except for a strategically placed, oversized tie. (Harry was a major advertiser and I wondered whether *The Globe and Mail's* publisher would kill me. He didn't. But Mrs. Rosen almost did.)

I loved helping run the newspaper and remember that when I was asked to become a full-time columnist instead, it almost seemed a comedown. I've learned, however, that few things in life are completely accidental. Recently I had lunch with a friend who is a talented psychiatrist. "Tell me about yourself," he said sneakily, and so I told him about growing up in the suburbs of Chicago, where my first exposure to journalism was the *Chicago Tribune*. I adored a certain columnist named Mike Royko, a tough-talking, cigar-chomping guy who pulled no punches. One day I decided to call the phone number at the end of his column and tell him so. It took me days to get up the nerve, and I tried several times before I could will my trembling fingers to complete the call. "Royko here," said a gruff voice on the other end. It was all I could do to blurt out a compliment, before speedily hanging up. When I finished this story, my psychiatrist friend said, "Has it ever occurred to you that not many thirteen-year-old girls idolize a newspaper columnist?"

Columnists will tell you they have the best job in journalism, and it's true. The reason isn't just the soapbox—it's the personal connection we have with readers. My greatest reward is hearing from people who say, "You put my thoughts into words," or, "You've said what people think but are afraid to say." One frequently asked question is: "How long does it take you to write your column?" The answer is, a few hours, and around thirty years. First you have to learn the craft, which is the easy part. Then you have to have something to say. I've always worried that I might run out of things to say, that one day I'd wake up and make the ultimate withdrawal from the column bank. But I never have. Fortunately for me, we're not likely to run out of human folly and political stupidity anytime soon. They are the world's most renewable resources.

Lots of people tell me that they don't always agree with what I write but like reading me anyway. Some tell me they never agree, but they like getting their blood pressure up. (Many people have demanded that I be fired but so far the *Globe* has not obliged them.) I don't always agree with me either—especially when I look back with the wisdom of hindsight, and without the pressure of a deadline, at a particular story. That has been part of the pleasure of creating this book—being able to revisit some of the subjects that fascinate me the most, with the time and space to delve into them a little further.

A good column is like a good cup of coffee—stimulating, with just enough caffeine to wake you up and get you thinking. But a book is a whole pot of coffee. It's something you can sit back with and savour at your leisure.

Margaret Wente

May 2009

Chapter One

You Can't *Say* That!

The in-box is the most entertaining, illuminating and humbling part of my job. That's how I know who's cheering, who's jeering, and who would like to draw and quarter me. That's how I have learned (the hard way) about the most cherished beliefs of my fellow citizens.

"I just read your recent article, and I happened to be shocked and appalled by your countless referrals to the Wiccan community," wrote one indignant reader, a student who identified herself as a Psychology and Religions major. "I'm not holding my breath on a respose [*sic*] from you. The important thing is that you've read this, and it will aggrivate [*sic*] you."

Well, spelling doesn't really count for much in higher education these days. Nor does a sense of irony. My reference to the Wiccans was a humorous (I thought) effort to demonstrate how extremely respectful we have become about one another's religious beliefs, however marginal those beliefs may be. But in Canada, it seems, you don't have to go out of your way to offend someone. It just happens naturally.

"You are so out of touch with reality it is truly sad," wrote another reader. "In my opinion, you have abused your position and you should be requested to apologize to the public for misleading them. Your columns are purely editorial, with your information gathered from your coffee buddies in Toronto." Or, as someone else succinctly put it: "You Are A Looser [*sic*]!"

A lot of readers think I'm far too rude in print. But many of them don't beat around the bush either. After I criticized a former *Globe* columnist named Heather Mallick for some of her more bizarre views, a Mallick fan mailed me a postcard that said, "Although I did not always agree with her opinions, she is much better than you. Her book is also more interesting than yours." Ouch!

I seem to have a special talent for offending underdogs and minority groups. These have included Muslims, elderly drivers, feminists, Newfoundlanders, AIDS activists, and people who think our Greatest Canadian is David Suzuki. I routinely offend people who dislike elitists. Perhaps my favourite letter of all time came in response to a column I wrote defending the right of the National Ballet to fire a dancer who was past her prime. The dancer in question was outraged, and threatened legal action on the grounds of discrimination. I argued that the National Ballet was all about excellence, and had the right to make its personnel decisions accordingly. But this is Canada. We don't go in for elitism here.

"Where are the aboriginal dancers and the dancers of colour?" one writer demanded to know. "Where are the dancers with disabilities?"

Since then, I've pondered what a truly egalitarian National

Ballet might look like. It would probably include fat dancers, one-legged dancers, and dancers who can't follow a tune. But after all, why shouldn't everybody have a chance?

People who take issue with my views don't write only to me, of course. They also write to the Letters page. Some days, the Letters editor needs a flame-retardant suit. I don't set out deliberately to be incendiary when I write. The idea is to provoke thinking and debate, not to lob grenades. But ours is a nation of fierce identity groups and ancient grievances. And from time to time I've really put my foot in it.

There was, for instance, the time I defended Dick Pound for saying that Canada had once been a nation of "savages." Actually, he said "*sauvages*," because the interview was in French. Mr. Pound, a Canadian member of the International Olympic Committee, was defending the choice of China for the 2008 Olympics. Despite human rights abuses, he argued, China was an ancient and sophisticated culture. By contrast, Canada, until four centuries ago, had been "*un pays de sauvages.*" The moment his interview was published, the S-word hit the fan.

"Mr. Pound must apologize to First Peoples and educate himself about the history of First Peoples in this country," insisted Phil Fontaine, national chief of the Assembly of First Nations. Other native groups demanded that he resign from the Vancouver Olympics organizing committee. Editorial writers roundly scolded him.

Not me. For some suicidal reason, I decided to argue that his tactless comment might not have been totally incorrect and that European civilization, in fact, *was* in many ways more advanced. I took a swipe at the currently accepted view of North America's past, before the Europeans came to wreck it. According to this account, the land was occupied by a race of gentle pastoralists with their own science, their own medicine and their own oral history that was every bit as rich and sophisticated as Europe's. The noble savage figure from the children's literature of my youth—think of Uncas, in *The Last of the Mohicans*—has been updated for a new generation. Today, it's the aboriginal peoples who are thought to have been wise and good, and it's the Europeans who are regarded as the savage ones. Historically, aboriginal peoples were more spiritual, more egalitarian, more peaceable, less greedy and more ecologically minded than the Europeans. And if you don't believe that, then you're just being culturally insensitive.

I said that, and much else. People were not happy. Several thousand of them signed on to a Facebook site called "Fire Margaret Wente." Hundreds shot off e-mails to the paper denouncing me for historical ignorance, racism, colonialism and general insensitivity. "Crudely provocative and blandly Eurocentric," wrote one, "heaps insult upon injury" said another, "[this] can only perpetuate the ignorance and mistruths . . . about First Nations people," claimed yet another. And those were the polite ones. What about the Europeans in the Americas "who went about murdering, raping and pillaging in the name of God and gold?" was a query echoed by many. Eminent scholars penned op-ed pieces in which they deplored my lack of knowledge. Hayden King, a professor of indigenous studies at McMaster University, wrote in the *Globe* that my column had "likely set back the First Nations campaign for an accurate representation of native peoples in the mainstream media by ten years." One "indigenous Canadian," however, did commend my candour for "shining a light on the dark underbelly of a troubling family history."

What did I learn? I learned how deeply entrenched the new mythology is—although, in a world where the residential schools disaster is now characterized as "genocide," I shouldn't have been. But I also learned other lessons. I learned that the power of a single word (*savages*) can blind people to everything else you have to say. "It's as if you were writing about seventeenth-century Jews, and called them 'moneylenders,'" says one woman I know. "That's factual in a way. But it can't help but sound offensive." I don't know how the reaction would' have differed if I'd simply left that word out. It was too provocative. And I should have known that.

The touchiest Canadians of all, however, live in Newfoundland. Newfoundlanders are a tribe like no other, with a collective sense of pride, grievances and memories that are almost as ancient as the Rock itself.

Newfoundlanders do not forget, and they are slow to forgive. Even today, whenever I speak in public, someone will pop up and say, "Aren't you sorry for what you wrote about Newfoundland?"

It all started with a piece I wrote back in 2005. At the time, Newfoundland's premier, Danny Williams, was quarrelling with the prime minister over oil royalties, and local tempers were running high. One day, as Newfoundlanders cheered wildly, Danny hauled down the Canadian flag in protest. And so I wrote a piece called "Oh Danny Boy, Pipe Down." And I have never heard the end of it. Neither have my editors.

Here it is.

In Newfoundland and Labrador, Danny Williams can do no wrong. These days, he's more popular than God. Following his lead, the people of the Rock have banished the Maple Leaf from their dominion. Angry citizens are flooding open-line shows and threatening that, unless they get what's owed to them by Canada, Newfoundland should go it alone.

My grandpa had a saying for moments like this. He would have said, "Here's your hat, what's your hurry?"

I like Newfoundlanders. I really do. But their sense of victimhood is unmatched. And their flag protest isn't winning them much sympathy on this side of the Gulf of St. Lawrence. In fact, the sensation on this side is of a deep and painful bite to the hand that feeds. Mr. Williams reminds me of a deadbeat brother-in-law who's hit you up for money a few times too often. He's been sleeping on your couch for years, and now he's got the nerve to complain that it's too lumpy.

The ins and outs of the current squabble between Newfoundland and Ottawa would baffle any normal human being. Technically, the fight is over the esoteric details of equalization payments and offshore revenues. But according to Mr. Williams, it's really about treachery, deceit and betrayal.

Peter Fenwick has a different view. Mr. Fenwick, a long-time Newfoundland political commentator, says it's about having your cake and eating it, too. "He's going to end up with a cake and a half," he says. "And he's got 95 percent of the province behind him."

Over the years, those of us not blessed to be born on the Rock have sent countless cakes its way in the form of equalization payments, pogey, and various hare-brained make-work schemes. (Who can ever forget the hydroponic cucumber farm?) In return, the surly islanders have blamed us for everything from the disappearance of the cod stocks to the destruction of the family unit, because if people had to work more than ten weeks before they could collect EI, they might have to move away.

This hallowed policy of siphoning money from the haves to the have-nots, so that everyone can be equal, has turned Canada into a permanently aggrieved nation, in which every region of the country is convinced that it's being brutally ripped off by every other region. No one is better at this blame game than the Newfs, egged on by generations of politicians. The only way to get elected there is to pledge to stop the terrible atrocities of Ottawa (i.e., not sending enough money). If you should make the error of suggesting that people might have to become more self-sufficient, your political career is dead. Politicians like to get elected, which is why things never change.

Newfoundland's population has dwindled to something less than that of Scarborough, Ontario. Because of stupendous political malfeasance, it is at least $11 billion in debt. But it still has seven federal seats. And so we send more money so that people can stay in the scenic villages where they were born, even though the fish are gone and there's no more work and never will be, unless they can steal some telemarketing from Bangalore. Rural Newfoundland (along with our great land north of "60") is probably the most vast and scenic welfare ghetto in the world.

But who can blame people for wanting to stay put? Not me. No one will ever gobble down a plate of cod tongues and pen an ode to Scarborough. Scarborough is not romantic. It is filled with ugly high-rise towers of immigrants scrambling to gain a foothold in a new land far from home. The difference is that, when they do it, we congratulate them and call it enterprise. No one will ever buy a scenic picture postcard of a strip mall. But Scarborough supports itself, and Newfoundland does not, and I wish Danny Williams would explain why it's a good idea to keep picking the pockets of Chinese dry cleaners and Korean variety-store owners who work ninety hours a week in order to keep subsidizing the people who live in Carbonear, no matter how quaint and picturesque they are.

I like Newfoundlanders, I really do. Where would we be without Rex Murphy and Mary Walsh and Rick Mercer? On the other hand, they left.

As for you other people of the Rock, maybe we can strike a deal. You can keep all the oil and gas revenues. And you can pay us back all the money we've sent you since you joined Confederation. Fair enough?

I thought not.

I might as well have saved some ink and just called them "savages." The column traded on every stereotype that Newfoundlanders had been saddled with for years. I knew that, of course. But what I didn't understand was the deeply rooted narrative that shapes a proud people's sense of their history. This narrative too contains a bedrock of truth—of a people and place exploited for centuries by outsiders, who took the wealth and left nothing but hardship and bitterness behind. If you don't understand this, then you don't understand Newfoundlanders—proud, prickly and mad as hell.

"You, my dear, are stunned as me arse," one reader wrote. That was among the more courteous responses. "I am a Newfoundlander, and damn proud of it" went a typical e-mail. "I do not receive welfare, or EI. I work forty hours per week and drive for two hours a day to get to and from my job. . . . Newfoundland is a

very proud province with an abundance of hard-working people."
Wrote another: "Racist remarks like yours about Newfoundland
can only be emitted from a very sad, unhappy, uninformed and
bitter person. At least that is what I tell my kids when they ask why
you wrote such hurtful things about the place that they love."

If flame mail could incinerate a computer, mine would be in
ashes. I heard from 2,500 people, and 98 percent of them wanted
to boil me in a vat of seal oil. One woman called me and burst
into tears. A high-school student called to ask if I was as offensive in person as I am in print. *The Globe and Mail*'s circulation in
Newfoundland is not all that high, and so the volume of e-mail
astonished me. I swear that some folks took out a subscription just
so they could cancel it in protest.

I hadn't really meant to say that Newfoundlanders are lazy welfare bums. My comments were meant to describe the province's
doleful economics, its history of bad policy leadership, and Mr.
Williams's theatrical shenanigans. But people on the island took it
personally, and I became a lightning rod for widespread resentment
against the condescension and paternalism of the mainland. "Their
sense of superiority and righteousness is incredible," wrote one
reader, referring to people like me. "The belief they are the 'hand
that feeds' is no different than the British colonialism that Newfoundland and Labrador endured for centuries."

For days, my piece was read aloud and condemned on radio
talk shows. It was reprinted and condemned in the St. John's *Tele-
gram*. I was denounced repeatedly by Mr. Williams, who refused
to appear on any program I was on. Teachers read my column
aloud to their classes as a prime example of racism and stereotyping.
On CBC–TV in St. John's, former federal cabinet minister John
Crosbie shouted me down. He reminded people how they'd been

robbed since the 1930s, called my column "racist," and blasted the "fat-cat elites" of Upper Canada. I found out that he has one accent when he's talking to the home crowd, and a completely different one when he addresses the mainland. From time to time, Mr. Crosbie has used language not unlike my own. In his memoir recalling his days in Ottawa, he accused more than one Newfoundland politician of "biting the hand that fed him so lavishly." He once told former premier Brian Peckford that Newfoundland's financial mess existed "despite the generous help of the government and the people of Canada." But that was a long time ago.

Newfoundlanders share a profound collective sense of their own history. They believe they've given far more to Canada than they've got back, and they're convinced they've been cheated out of what rightfully belongs to them. "You are completely ignorant of history," hundreds of people wrote. "For decades, you mainlanders have taken everything we had." To them, this is what the fight over resource revenues is really all about. As Brian Peckford told me, "It's about our place in Confederation. It's everything."

I learned other lessons, too. I learned just how passionate and proud is the attachment of Newfoundlanders to their home. That attachment makes the rest of us look rootless. They grieve for all of those who've had to leave, and many of those who've left will always regard themselves as exiles.

"Newfoundland is the most beautiful place in the world and the reason we are still on this beautiful island is because we have to work like dogs to be here," wrote one person. For all its hardships, they think life in Newfoundland is better than life anywhere else. "The way I see it, you wish you were a Newfoundlander instead of living in disease-infested Ontario," another wrote.

A handful of people (generally those who had left home to find work in the oil patch of Alberta) said they agreed with me. But mostly, they echoed the sentiments of the man who wrote: "You should be slapped with a cod and drenched in screech." My legacy is still a plague to every *Globe and Mail* reporter—indeed, any reporter from Toronto—who finds herself there on assignment. No, she must constantly explain, she doesn't share my views, and she doesn't even know me.

Only a few weeks after my effigy was boiled in seal oil, however, a tremor rattled the streets of St. John's. Margaret Wente was said to be in town. I had become infamous, and so reporters were dispatched to hunt me down.

In fact, Margaret Wente *was* in town. The other one. The other Margaret Wente is my niece, Maggie. She is a young Toronto lawyer whose views differ from mine in almost every way. She bears the curse of my name.

"Good God, woman, have you considered changing your name?" a friend e-mailed her from St. John's. "It's most unfortunate for you to be a Wente in this province at this time."

When she checked in to her hotel in St. John's, Maggie had to explain that she wasn't me.

"Oh, we were waiting for her!" the desk clerk said. "We were so excited! We were going to be really, really nice to her. We're nice to everyone. That's the way Newfoundlanders are. But I'm kind of glad it's not her."

"Your name was everywhere," marvelled Maggie. "People were quoting from your column. They gave you credit for rallying people behind Danny Williams."

After Maggie checked in, her phone started ringing off the hook. She kept explaining that she wasn't me. But she was big news anyway. "Margaret Wente hits St. John's!" blared the local radio station, before revealing that it wasn't me. Reporters asked her how she was being treated, and what she thought about my views. She told them that her views weren't the same as mine. This made news, too. Soon I started getting e-mails saying, "Even your own niece thinks you're a jerk!"

As Maggie was unpacking, there was a knock on the door. It was room service, with a huge plate of cheese and fruit for the other Margaret Wente. When Maggie said she wasn't me, they said, "Never mind, we want you to have it anyway. We're kind of happy you're not her."

Maggie wound up having a terrific time in Newfoundland. She was a celebrity everywhere she went, even though (or especially because) she wasn't me. In the town of Clarenville, a couple of hours' drive from St. John's, she met someone who was so thrilled to meet somebody named Margaret Wente that he asked her home for supper.

"Guess who I brought home!" he told his wife. His wife was one of the several thousand people who had written a furious e-mail to me. "You'll never guess who's sitting in our living room!" she exclaimed to a friend who phoned. They were all relieved to discover that one of us Wentes, at least, is a decent human being, and said they hoped she'd come back soon.

Still, Maggie would rather not be mistaken for me. "If my parents had realized how notorious you'd become, they would have considered naming me something else."

As for me, I've solved the problem that's been weighing heavily on my mind: I won't have to change my name the next time I go to Newfoundland. I'll just pretend I'm her.

———

A lot has happened since 2005. Danny Billions was re-elected by an overwhelming 83 percent majority. And now the shoe is on the other foot. Newfoundland struck oil, and for the first time in its history, it is a "have" province. And guess who's a have-not? That would be poor, old, oil-less Ontario. The day Ontario officially became a "have-not province," my in-box filled up all over again with gleeful letters from the people of the Rock. Here's a typical message:

> How does it feel to reside in a Have Not Province?????
> OMG, it looks so good on you to fall on hard times and
> be the poor relative. I laughed my ass off when I heard that
> Ontario is now classified as a have-not province and will
> now have to accept "cakes" from Newfoundland. Hope you
> are not whining about it. I could go on but I'm sure you
> get the point. Not many Newfoundlanders will forget your
> cruel and uninformed editorial.
>   Eileen from Newfoundland and Labrador
>   HAVE PROVINCE

My own former fat-cat province of Ontario still sends billions more to Ottawa than it gets back. But nobody feels sorry for us. So, Danny! If you ever need a job, please think of us.

Chapter Two

Where Did All My Money Go?

As the economic news went from bad to catastrophic over the past year, it seemed like everybody in business circles was reading a book called *The Black Swan: The Impact of the Highly Improbable.* The black swan is the bird that was thought not to exist, because no one had ever seen one. Then black swans turned up in Australia, proving that the most knowledgeable ornithologists were completely wrong.

"Remember that ten-year plan we used to have?" I asked my husband. "The black swan just pooped all over it."

Our friends are all in the same boat. They diligently gathered food for the winter of their lives and stashed it away in a safe place. They didn't gamble it away or blow it on expensive toys (except, maybe, for the odd forty-inch TV). They paid down their debt. They bought and held. They were proud of being ants, not grasshoppers.

"Why weren't we grasshoppers?" I complained to my husband.

"Think of all the fun we could have had. I could have owned a Prada. We could have had a Beemer. We could have stayed at the Four Seasons and ordered breakfast in bed."

The lesson of the black swan is that the world is governed not by ordinary and predictable events but by extraordinary and unpredictable ones. The asteroid that wiped out the dinosaurs is an example of a black swan. The Internet is a good black swan, the crash of '08 a bad one. Except for one or two eccentric cranks, no one saw it coming. But I should have had a glimmer. Whenever I start gloating over my piggy bank, the end is nigh.

"Honey," I said to my husband just over a year before the market went south. "Our RRSPs have gone up. Our house has gone up. We're rich! We won't be eating cat food in our old age after all."

My husband never counts up our money. He's too superstitious. He is self-employed, and always thinks his current job might be his last. "We may be eating cat food," he said. "But it will be premium cat food."

Then came the meltdown. One day after the stock market went down nearly 900 points, I left a message on his cellphone. "Hi, honey," I said. "It's not so bad. At least we have each other."

Suddenly we were feeling poor, even though we're not. We haven't lost our house or jobs. There are no villains at our door demanding that we pay the rent. All our losses are entirely on paper, and even then they aren't so very much. But we immediately thought, shouldn't we be starting to economize?

It seems like only yesterday that we were giddy with glee over skyrocketing house prices in our neighbourhood. When a For Sale sign went up outside a spiffy new stone house a few doors up the street we rushed on to the Internet to find out how much it was listed for.

"A million five," guessed my husband.

"Guess again," I said. "Try two million five."

We shrieked with laughter at the hubris of it all. The highest price ever paid for a house on our street was a million six, and we thought *that* was insane. Three days later a Sold sign went up. The house went for $2.45 million.

We were shocked. But really, we were thrilled. Twenty years before, my husband had bought the modest little place we live in for what then seemed like a lot of money. He figured it was worth it because it was near the lake. Back then the housing stock in Toronto's Beaches area was distinctly middle class—single-storey cottages and homely brick or wooden semis, with a sprinkling of grand old turreted wooden mansions. The people who lived there were teachers, minor bank managers and Volvo drivers from the CBC.

Now our neighbours are investment bankers, top accountants and successful info/entertainment entrepreneurs. They drive Jaguars and Land Rovers. Our creaky little cottage is flanked by hulking new stone mansions crammed onto fifty-foot lots. They have master bedrooms with his-and-her ensuites, bathrooms with heated floors, entrances with floating staircases, and kitchens with Sub-Zero refrigerators. The people in them can't survive in less than 3,500 square feet. Sometimes I think of the little one-bathroom bungalow my parents lived in with three kids, and wonder how we managed.

A day after the big stone house went on the market, so did an old wreck on the same block. It was being sold for its redevelopment potential. The asking price—for a lot measuring 50 by 120 feet, the same size as ours—was absurd. My husband and I killed ourselves laughing. Within a week it sold for $1.05 million.

"Congratulations," I said to my husband. "We own a million-dollar teardown."

With our country house increasingly seeming like home, we were beginning to think that maybe it was time to downsize in the city. And, suddenly, it seemed as if everyone we knew was buying a condo. After years of accumulating more and more, they wanted less and less. Mostly, they wanted less to mow and shovel and re-roof and repaint. They wanted to live right downtown where they wouldn't have to drive. I could see their point. I thought it would be fun to live in a glass house in the sky and throw stones.

"Maybe we should think about moving to a condo," I told my husband.

He was not so keen. "Over my dead body," he said.

He likes our scruffy old house. But the peer pressure was getting to me. I found myself devouring the condo ads the way other people consume porn. I couldn't resist projecting myself into a sleek, glass-walled penthouse, with the city at my feet. There I would be a more sophisticated and more worldly version of me, with better furniture.

Coincidentally, we have a friend who is a condo lawyer. We call her the Condo Queen because she knows everything about them. One day I asked her for advice about buying a condo. "Don't do it!" she said. She herself doesn't live in a condo. She lives in a nice house with a big backyard.

Still, the moment comes when the Zeitgeist overtakes you. I know this moment well. It's the moment when you start to think you want to rent a house in France and discover that everybody else is renting a house in France, too. This only makes you even more anxious to rent a house in France right this very minute, before they run out of them. Belonging to the Boomer generation is like that. It's like belonging to a giant school of fish. All the fish turn left or right at precisely the same time, as if guided by a single reflex. Each fish thinks it has free will, but that is an illusion. I kept showing my husband condo listings, but he refused to bite.

"I don't understand condos," he would say. "I don't understand why they cost $750 a square foot. I don't understand why a shoe-box with glass walls is worth more than our entire house and our backyard, and why you have to pay extra for the parking space."

I didn't know why either. Still, I could tell he was beginning to weaken. We agreed that in the unlikely event that we ever did get serious about a condo, it would have to have great views, low management fees and not too many frills. Why pay for fancy marketing campaigns, a concierge, a yoga room and other amenities we have no use for? Also, we would never buy from plans.

Two days after we had this heart-to-heart, we bought a condo with indifferent views and high management fees. The marketing campaign was very fancy. There will be a concierge, a yoga room and other amenities we have no use for. It was to be ready within two years, or maybe three or four. Naturally, we bought from plans.

"Ha, ha, ha-ha-ha," said the Condo Queen when I broke the news to her. "You bunnies."

But I didn't care. Every so often I would go and look at the hole in the ground, and dream of how fabulous our new lives would be.

When I showed the sales contract to the Condo Queen, she burst out laughing. "This floor plan doesn't even have the room dimensions on it!" she said. The advertised completion date, she warned, was just a come-on. Maybe our condo would be ready before it was time to move into the old-age home. Or maybe not. Maybe it would be bigger than a shoebox. Or maybe not.

"Don't worry," said a friend of ours, an interior designer. "It's a very efficient use of space."

"Take the time to the completion date and double it," advised someone else I know, whose condo was two years late. By that time he'd been transferred to California, and had to sell it.

We bought the condo partly because we know some other people who'd bought a condo in that building, and we think they're smart. Whenever we ran into them, we would tell each other what a wise decision we had made. Later, I was told, we would bond even more when we sued the developer. Everyone winds up suing the developer.

A few months later we got a letter from the condo people. It said that if we wanted any wiring or mechanical changes, we had to tell them right away. "Have you done your lighting plan yet?" asked the people we know who had bought number 2905. I had never heard of a lighting plan, so I asked them what it was. They explained that if we wanted another pot light, or wanted to move the fixture in the dining room, we had to decide now.

"You must be kidding," I said. "How am I supposed to know?"

That was just the start. Were we planning to get the automated window coverings, so we could flick a switch to make the shades go up and down? What about a fireplace, a gas stove, a wine fridge? What about the reading lights in our bedroom?

I began to panic. The place wouldn't even be ready for another two or three years. "Help," I said to Melody, the interior designer. "I need a lighting plan, whatever that is." She asked to see my wiring and ceiling diagrams. I said I didn't know there were such things. She got the condo people to e-mail them over. They were full of dotted lines and symbols I couldn't understand, and she pronounced them shockingly inadequate. She made a detailed list of changes and sent them to a terrifying person named Bernard, who works for the condo people. His main job is to say "no" in a very refined accent. His other job is to inform you that if you want an extra pot light, the cost will be $3,000.

In other words, the stupendous price we paid for our glass box was just a starting point. Parking space? That will be an extra $39,000. Locker? $8,000. There are other extras, called "upgrades," which are available only through the official condo people. How about a small wine fridge? That will run us $7,000. Those auto-mated shades? $25,000. When I told the Condo Queen she was scandalized. "Drapes!" she said. "Get drapes!"

At the rate we're going, even drapes might be a stretch. I have a vision of us lounging by the full-length glass windows in our undies, swilling our too-warm wine for all to see. We could be quite old by then.

"I get the sense that they're really behind schedule," the Condo Queen told me. My husband didn't mind, though. In fact, he was as happy as a clam. If the condo wasn't built yet, that was good, because he figured that the value of our house would probably keep going up. By the time we had to sell it, we'd get more than enough money to pay for the condo. That, of course, was all B.M. (Before Meltdown) thinking. Now the selling price of our house will hardly cover what we still owe on the condo—far less the extras. "Maybe we don't really need a Sub-Zero fridge," I said to my husband. But according to our condo contract, we're stuck.

Like us, all our friends are worried about the new cracks in their nest eggs. They know that nothing is likely to go up again for a while, only sideways or down. Some are wondering what will hap-pen to their pension plans, and some are afraid that they'll outlive their money. It doesn't matter how affluent they are. They're all feeling poor.

We are luckier than a lot of folks we know. My husband is a Scot, and I am half a Scot on my mother's side. This means that we are genetically allergic to debt. I know for a fact that if we don't pay off our Visa bills every month, we will go to hell. Suddenly this quaint old-time religion is back in fashion, like bell-bottoms. We're feeling trendy for the first time in thirty-five years.

We also know that we are rich beyond our grandparents' wildest dreams. We like to think that's because we work hard and are smart. But really, it's because we won the lottery. The economy had been on a roll for years. We bought houses in Toronto way back when they were cheap, and planned to reap a windfall from one of the greatest real-estate run-ups of all time. Now those happy days are gone, and the housing market has grown cold. Despite some upticks in the stock market, the recession in the United States looks to be long and hard. There is a silver lining, though. The bloated financial industry will shrink back to its proper size. The best and brightest of our sons and daughters will no longer be sucked up by the fast-money world of investment banking. Maybe some of them will decide to be doctors or teachers instead. Some might even make things.

Well, I've learned my lesson. Never, ever will I gloat over our piggy bank. Never again will I congratulate myself on how much our house must be worth. Just don't ask me to look at our investment statements for a while. I'd rather slip them in the bottom drawer and try to forget they're there.

A friend who has read the black swan book says we're learning that we have far less influence over the universe than we thought. The black swan teaches us that what we've learned from the past is, at best, irrelevant and, at worst, viciously misleading.

Still, I'd like to strangle that damn bird.

Chapter Three

Crash of the Titans

Who says Canadians are dull? Although we may have a reputation as the world's most innocuous people, we also have our share of characters with personalities larger than life.

Conrad Black and Brian Mulroney are the two who fascinate me the most. Both had soaring ambition, stupendous gifts, titanic egos and fatal flaws. Both have been admired and reviled in equal measure, and both have left me feeling deeply conflicted. At the peak of their influence and renown, they both committed entirely unnecessary acts that ruined their reputations and exposed them as venal and greedy. They were smart, successful men who did phenomenally stupid things. Both are now grappling with public disgrace.

And both are certain that history will vindicate them.

Why did they do it? Brian Mulroney didn't need the few hundred thousand dollars in cash that he took from a sleazy lobbyist, and Conrad Black certainly didn't need the few million dollars he squeezed from shareholders. Was it simply greed? Or was it some fatal flaw in judgment that took them down? Although I know them both a little bit, I've never had the guts to ask them.

————

Many people cheered the downfall of Conrad Black, but I wasn't one. It's hard to dislike a man who's nice to your little sister. My sister lives in Chicago, where Conrad Black sat through a four-month trial that ended in his conviction. I was there for parts of it, and invited her to drop in. She'd told me she was dying to meet Conrad. She showed up in her favourite outfit—frayed blue jeans, sneakers and a hoodie—and when recess came I introduced them in the hall. "My sister is a keen student of Chicago history," I said.

At that, his eyes lit up. "Chicago's flag is quite fascinating," he observed, like someone without a care in the world. He's six foot four and my sister is five foot two, so he practically had to stoop to talk to her. "It has four stars on it to mark four great events. I recall what three of them are but I'm not certain of the fourth."

I held my breath and wondered if my sister would be any match for Conrad Black and his prodigious memory.

"The fourth star represents the Century of Progress Exposition of 1933–34," she said, and from then on they were soulmates. They ignored me and chatted merrily away about the history of the park system, until his lawyer dragged him back into court.

My sister has a wicked sense of humour. As soon as Conrad was out of sight, she unzipped her hoodie and showed me the T-shirt she was wearing underneath. "*Alcatraz*," it said in giant letters. "I was dying to take my jacket off and show it to him. He's been a naughty, naughty man."

I've met Conrad here and there for more than twenty years, ever since he wrote a column for the business magazine I once edited at the *Globe*. (I am among the few people in the world who can say they were once Conrad Black's boss.) He's an amazing man. His memory is near-photographic. He can name all the British ships that fought in the Battle of Trafalgar, and he can also recall where he last had lunch with you nine years ago, who else was there and what you discussed. He is courteous to servants and strangers, a habit you can't always count on among the very rich.

Lord Black was in many ways an anachronism in the world of business—a throwback to the days when merchants called themselves "proprietors" and when "transparency" was a desirable aspect of plastic wrap. His entry into the business establishment was sponsored by Bud McDougald, the man who ran the Argus conglomerate, described by Peter Newman as the most successful nest-feathering operation in the country. Mr. Black took over Argus at the tender age of thirty-eight, in a coup that established him as a brilliant but devious business strategist. He even dressed like an anachronism—buttoned up in formal pinstripe suits at a time when most other men his age were loosening their ties.

Even then, he was converting his family home into the grandest mansion on Toronto's Bridle Path and wintering with the moneyed class in Palm Beach. Controversy dogged his business ventures from the start. And from the start, he has dismissed his critics as envious, spiteful and small-minded. Until the end, he acted as if he had never, not even for a moment, contemplated the possibility of jail time. And after that, he acted as if his conviction had been a dreadful mistake that was certain to be overturned on appeal. He kept assuring friends that the monumental injustices done to him would be certain to transform corporate governance on a global scale.

Conrad is a masterly and persuasive speaker, and before his trial he had persuaded much of Toronto society that U.S. federal prosecutors were engaged in a grotesque McCarthyesque witch hunt. If anyone had looted the company, he insisted, it wasn't him. It was his partner, David Radler.

Mr. Radler squeezed the *Chicago Sun–Times,* the ninth largest newspaper in the United States, exactly the same way he squeezed Hollinger's small-town papers. He turned off the escalators to save money. Then he shut down one of the elevators. The phone system was one step above two tin cans with string. The editorial budget was cut to the bone, and then some. Meanwhile, Mrs. Black, who rarely ventured into the building, was collecting more than $100,000 a year for her editorial advice. The money barely covered the cost of her Manolos.

And it was the shoes (and what went with them) that brought them down. If Mr. and Mrs. Black had led a life of slightly less conspicuous consumption, the shareholders at the investment firm Tweedy, Browne, which owned a big chunk of Hollinger, might not have started asking pesky questions. They might never have begun wondering why Mr. Black was dressing up like Cardinal Richelieu and styling himself Lord Black of Crossharbour, whatever that meant, while David Radler was running the *Sun–Times* into the ground. If Lady Black had never posed for that eight-page spread in *Vogue,* featuring a tour of her couture collection, or confessed that "my extravagance knows no bounds," then Lord Black might not be in the slammer today. They were obviously doing very, very well, and the shareholders were not. And that is how their troubles started.

As it all began to unravel, Mrs. Black sent an e-mail to the then editor of the *Sun–Times,* Mike Cook. She assured Mr. Cook that she had always been there to advise him on any editorial matters—

and asked him to send her an e-mail back to confirm, for the record, that this was true. The bean-counters, meantime, had asked her husband to reimburse the company for a trip the couple took to Bora Bora on the corporate jet. Mr. Black was not inclined to do so. "Needless to say, no such outcome is acceptable," he replied.

Canada's white-collar crime investigators operate at a stately, even snail-like pace, and had Black been charged in Canada, it's likely that we'd still be waiting for his day in court. But he had renounced his Canadian citizenship in order to become a lord. He tried to get it back again, because, as his lawyer said, he "loves Canada." Alas, it was too late. He had to face American justice after all.

Back in 2005, I ran into Lord and Lady Black at a large party in a charming old farmhouse in the country outside Toronto. Nobody with whom they used to socialize had seen them in years. But now they were in trouble, and, after dazzling social careers in London and New York, had retreated to the backwater of Toronto, where they had set out to mount a charm offensive. They looked over-dressed and out of place amid the local gentry. "Where *are* we, actually?" asked Barbara plaintively. I waded through the crush, stuck out my hand and greeted her cordially. She reacted as if I were invisible, and coolly turned her back. Now, I thought, I know what it's like to be cut dead.

I couldn't blame her. I had once written that few women in the world could afford to dress like Lady Black, and that she, perhaps, was not among them. For a woman who was about to turn sixty-five, however, she looked extraordinarily good. "The trick is to get your 'work' done a little at a time, instead of all at once," she once told a friend of mine. She reminded me of Dorian Gray's sister.

If the Lord and Lady have a motto on their coat of arms, surely it is: "Never Surrender." Never surrender to the federal prosecutors, nor to prison, nor to all the petty little people who want to bring you down.

One of those people was Peter C. Newman—Canada's chronicler of the rich and famous, betrayer of confidences, and gossip extraordinaire. Nearly thirty years ago, Mr. Newman wrote a book called *The Establishment Man,* which turned Mr. Black into Canada's first genuine business celebrity. Mr. Newman's 2004 autobiography, *Here Be Dragons: Telling Tales of People, Passion and Power,* was far less kind. It was full of scurrilous anecdotes about Conrad's Hollinger International, and it spilled the dirt on Barbara's lurid (pre-Conrad) love life.

At a Toronto gala thrown by *Maclean's* magazine in 2005, the Blacks stole the show by having Mr. Newman (who was also in the room) served with a libel notice. It wasn't hard for the process server to spot him, since, as usual, he was wearing his Greek fisherman's hat. Loathing of the man in the fisherman's hat is something Conrad Black and Brian Mulroney have in common—Peter C. Newman has told nasty tales about them both. Mr. Newman, of course, peddles gossip for a living, and has done extremely well by it. At eighty, he remains extraordinarily prolific, perhaps on account of all the money he owes his ex-wives.

Mr. Newman's harsh reporting of Conrad Black's business dealings didn't shock insiders. One editor at the *Sun–Times* said, "I think it's a very charitable assessment, frankly. 'Rape and pillage' is how we're describing it here."

A few weeks before the trial started in 2007, I ran into Mr. Black once again. He told me he was confident that the citizens of Chicago would render a just verdict. When the time came, the nine women and three men waded through a complicated case and delivered a finely calibrated verdict. They rejected the overreaching charge of racketeering. They ignored the lifestyle crimes—the birthday party at La Grenouille, the trip to Bora Bora and all the rest. They zeroed in on the real meat-and-potatoes of the case—the obvious self-dealing, in which Conrad and Co. skimmed off non-compete payments the sellers didn't want, and paid them to themselves. The jury was also persuaded by a damning video that showed Lord Black skulking like a thief into his own office to cart away some mysterious boxes. We never did find out what was in them.

In the jury's eyes, the magnitude of Lord Black's crimes came closer to Martha Stewart's than to those of the WorldCom or Enron execs. This was no $450-million fraud, as one accuser had insisted, or even a $60-million fraud, as the prosecution insisted. In the end, the jury found him guilty for defrauding the shareholders of $6.5 million—not peanuts, but not enough to merit decades in prison, either.

Unfortunately for Lord Black, he's no Martha Stewart. Never, never, never will he admit his guilt or appear contrite. He will never emerge from prison wearing a humble hand-knit poncho. And unlike Martha, he will never regain any of his business empire or his wide circle of famous and important friends. Martha Stewart has learned what Conrad Black has not. She now understands that whether or not she herself feels wronged is irrelevant. She learned the hard way that times have changed, and corporate practices now come under a different kind of scrutiny. She learned that even the smartest person can't outwit the tides of history. For a brilliant student of history like Mr. Black, his conviction was a fatally strange miscalculation.

Given the tenor of the times, Lord Black was lucky to get six and a half years in jail—a year or so for every million dollars that he kept from the shareholders. Justice was done. Yet, there was something to dissatisfy everyone about this case. The defence law-yers, including top gun Eddie Greenspan, collected a whopping $100 million in fees, but they lost. Although the prosecutors won, in the end their mountain of malfeasance amounted to a mouse. A $500-million fraud shrank to $60 million, then $30 million, and finally $6 million, an amount that must be substantially less than the cost of adding Lord Black's head to their trophy wall. They demanded twenty years, and got a third of that.

Nor will Lord Black's incarceration serve a larger social purpose. Compared to the scale of the current meltdown and the thefts of Bernie Madoff, Lord Black's larcenies were trivial. Ironically, the shareholders he abused would be far better off today if his crimes had never come to light. His mighty media empire was devoured by the scandal, and they lost everything.

Conrad Black is suffering a harsh punishment but seems to be bearing it rather well. He doesn't really care what you and I think of him. He knows that he's an innocent man, and that history will exonerate him. Maybe that's why he looks so serene, even when he's photographed in the jailhouse courtyard wearing sweat-pants with his shirt-tail out. Some people predicted, or perhaps hoped, that the hardships and humiliations of a prison routine would destroy his spirit. They were wrong. Prison, he reported in an e-mail, is "better than I had expected . . . more of a sociological laboratory than I had foreseen." He passes his time working in the library, giving history lectures to the other inmates, and writing his great *J'accuse*—a thunderous indictment of the U.S. justice vigilan-tes and the shareholders'-rights zealots who brought him down. In his own mind he's not a crook, he's a martyr.

Lord Black's powers of self-delusion—which allow him to stay optimistic in the face of all the odds—are common among highly successful men. His wife, Barbara Amiel Black, was always more realistic about the outcome of her husband's trials. "I am a North London Jew who has read a bit of history," she once wrote. "This means I know this: In a century that has seen the collapse of the Austro-Hungarian, British and Soviet empires, reversal of fortune is the rich bitch's reality."

Since then she has cast herself as an exile and an outsider, although, as she acknowledges, "being exiled to opulent Palm Beach is not exactly hard labour." She has described how she tried to chew off the supports for her bra when they set off the prison's metal detector, and how she hates her tormentors (including yours truly). "Every year," she writes, "forgiveness becomes more difficult, and now I'm close to the point where it's simply not on. I'm inclined to bargain and ask if it's all right to stop wanting to disembowel with my own hands those who have wronged my husband."

Always a fan of red-blooded American capitalism, Barbara has also developed an unlikely affection for the female underclass, many of whom also have a mate in jail. "The government takes away most every little thing they had one way or another during the persecution process, reduces them to rubble, and in a victim-oriented society they don't count much because they're hitched to a victimizer—though one-third of their men are probably innocent," she wrote in *Maclean's* after Conrad's incarceration.

Her staunch loyalty to her husband has flummoxed all her critics. They were sure she'd dump him. After all, Barbara Amiel has traded in husbands for better models the way other people trade in their cars. But she's a senior citizen now and she has a serious, chronic illness. Her fate (and her legal troubles) are intertwined with his, and she has stayed true. It's obvious that she has taken her husband's downfall far harder than he has. As she wrote shortly before his sentencing: "I am reliving Edgar Allan Poe's 'The Pit and the Pendulum,' a story that has given me nightmares since childhood. The blade swings lower and lower over the bound body, the red-hot walls of the cell move in closer to squash the victim, and the only escape is the unknown horror in the rat-filled pit."

Amid the melee on the courthouse steps after his sentencing, Lord Black looked impeccably serene. He is a man of faith, and he believes he's right with God. He is determined to bear his martyrdom with grace, like the saints of the early Catholic Church who were pierced with arrows, flayed alive or roasted on a spit. Nothing shakes him, for his conscience is at ease.

From the time he stole that school exam and sold the answers to the other kids—then blamed the teachers—he has possessed a remarkable ability to recast his life's events so that he is the persecuted hero. In the drama of his life, he is the large man, assaulted time and time again by hordes of vengeful pygmies. It is this arrogance that blinded him to the world around him, that led him to make stupid mistakes and fatal misjudgments. Anyone with a less titanic ego would have admitted error and said "sorry" long ago.

But not Conrad. It's not in his nature. He knows that he is right and the world is wrong, and that the verdict of history will come down on his side.

———

Although he was among the best prime ministers of recent times, Brian Mulroney remains, without doubt, the most reviled figure in Canadian political life. For that alone you've got to feel for him. People took a dislike to him long before his reputation was forever tarnished by news of his relationship with a sleazy lobbyist who gave him cash in plain brown envelopes.

Somehow, a few years back, I got on Mr. Mulroney's Rolodex. I think I was there by default, to be phoned when nobody else was home. He would call me whenever the latest round of headlines (cruelly unfair, in his view) erupted in *The Globe and Mail* or on the CBC. "It's all because of Stevie Cameron," he'd complain in that unctuous baritone, which tends to leave the public with the unfortunate impression that he's trying to pull a fast one. "She's been waging a vendetta against me for years."

He wasn't wrong about that. Stevie Cameron, a former reporter with the *Globe,* published several books trying to prove that Mulroney was mixed up in a scandal involving the purchase of some Airbus jets. She even became an undercover informant for the RCMP in hopes of smoking out a smoking gun. Although she never did get her man, she persuaded millions of Canadians that Mr. Mulroney must be guilty of something or other.

Although I only met the former prime minister once or twice, I spoke with him often, and I came to think of him as The Voice. He phoned me from his sickbed, from Washington on the morning of Ronald Reagan's funeral, and from an airport on his way to China. He never told me anything particularly newsworthy, but he was always entertaining. He is a superb (though self-involved) raconteur, a partisan politician to his toes, and an accomplished gossip with a keen eye for the foibles of his rivals.

After his near-fatal bout with pancreatitis in 2005, The Voice became weak and raspy. Once or twice, he called me late in the evening and told me what a close call he'd had. He told me that one dreadful night in the hospital, he dreamed that he had died, and that he was observing his own funeral as his son Ben delivered the eulogy. He struggled back to consciousness and begged Mila (who, as usual, was by his side) to call a doctor right away. It turned out that he *was* dying, and prompt medical attention saved his life. His recovery was slow. For weeks he wasn't allowed to make phone calls, although he cheated. As soon as he felt good enough he asked for his favourite food—a smoked-meat sandwich from Schwartz's in Montreal. We agreed that the restorative properties of a Schwartz's smoked-meat sandwich could not possibly be surpassed.

Not long afterwards, I, too, was in a hospital in Montreal, getting a new hip. The day after my surgery, the phone rang. It was The Voice. "Peggy, how are you doing?" he said. I said I was doing fine. The next day a man showed up at my bedside with a large paper bag. It was Brian Mulroney's driver, bearing two smoked-meat sandwiches from Schwartz's.

——————

When Brian Mulroney became prime minister, he agreed that Peter Newman would be the official chronicler of his time in office. For years, he sat with Mr. Newman and gave him the inside scoop—his real, unvarnished thoughts about the people and events of the day. Peter Newman taped it all. And then he published the tapes.

Mr. Newman's publication of his Mulroney tapes in 2005 revealed both men behaving pretty much in character. The first rule in public life is that a journalist is not your friend. Yet Mr. Mulroney vainly thought he'd charmed a journalist and made a friend of someone who would draw a sympathetic portrait of him for posterity. Given the way Mr. Newman had once eviscerated Diefenbaker, you've got to marvel at such a spectacularly suicidal lapse of judgment. But even Mr. Mulroney's friends admit that he can be his own worst enemy.

Mr. Newman was just doing what comes naturally—for him. "We non-fiction writers," he wrote in his autobiography, "can never be tamed or domesticated; only rented on occasion, but never bought. Those of us who have gained some measure of credibility practising this mad craft thrive on a pretend intimacy that spawns betrayal. However friendly an interview, however intimate the revelations, we writers remain temporary sojourners in a strange land. . . . I grovelled to pry open the Canadian Establishment's secrets but I never told them mine."

If this is what they're teaching in J-school these days, then I don't blame people for hating the media. Acting friendly toward your subject is just good journalistic practice, but Mr. Newman went way beyond the friendly interview. For many years, he ingratiated himself with the Mulroneys. They dined at each other's houses. Mila and Brian went to his wedding (one of them, at any rate) and helped scrape him off the floor after his divorce (I don't know which one). He gave Mila family heirlooms as sentimental presents. Not all their chats took place in the office with a tape recorder on the table. Many of them were casual evening phone calls, the fruit of Mr. Mulroney's incurable telephonophilia. Judging by what I know of Mr. Newman, you can bet the low gossip flowed in both directions.

Despite his protestations of innocence, there's an element of sleaze in what Mr. Newman did, and he knows it. Nor could he resist a final twist of the knife. Just before *The Secret Mulroney Tapes* hit the bookstores he had an autographed copy delivered to the Mulroneys' door with an inscription that read, *To Brian—At last Canadians will see you for the warm, funny and human person that you are—Peter.* There was also a patronizing little note: *I am so glad that you are feeling better. My wife Alvy was a nurse and described to me the agonizing pain you must have suffered. With best wishes to Mila for your continuing recuperation—and my blessings—Peter.*

Mr. Newman's tell-all didn't do much to move the needle of public opinion on his victim. For better or for worse, most people's opinions of Mr. Mulroney were already firmly set. But many of Mr. Mulroney's judgments recorded in the tapes struck me as about right. Clyde Wells was "the most unprincipled guy." Sheila Copps ("she'll never be a leader because she has no judgment") was a flake, and the Reform Party was never going to go anywhere because it was "anti-everything . . . it's all negative." He went overboard on Kim Campbell—it took both of them to reduce the party to two seats—but she relied far too much on her natural talent, and she ran a disastrous campaign. Mr. Mulroney, in fact, proved to have been a pretty astute judge of character—except when it came to himself. And then he got tangled up with a character named Karlheinz Schreiber.

And here's the story about the Schreiber affair that he has been telling for years to anyone who'll listen. After he left the prime minister's office in 1993, Mr. Mulroney says, he was virtually broke. He and Mila had used up all their savings while he was prime minister, and he left office poorer than when he entered it. He had a family and a big new mortgage. (What he didn't say was that he and Mila had social aspirations. They too wanted to hang around Palm Beach with people like the Blacks, and, to be fair, why shouldn't they?)

Mulroney had joined a Montreal law firm and was supposed to begin work after Labour Day. But he literally couldn't afford to wait. So he borrowed a secretary's desk and began his new job in the dog days of August—no longer a world leader, just a humble family man trying to put bread on the table. And so, when Karlheinz Schreiber came along with an envelope full of cash, he took it. It was, he says, the most colossal misjudgment of his life. At the time, he barely knew who Mr. Schreiber was. The payment was for legitimate business reasons. He declared the income and paid the taxes. He was just providing for his family.

Who could resist this charming tale? Not his many friends, his long-time aides and loyalists, his wide network of business associates, the many people he has helped and who genuinely like him. Besides, Mr. Mulroney was hounded for years, by the RCMP, the federal Department of Justice, the former Chrétien government, and journalists like Stevie Cameron and the CBC's *the fifth estate*.

The story of the cash payment—$300,000, according to Mr. Schreiber, although Mr. Mulroney says it was only $225,000—was disclosed in 2003 in *The Globe and Mail*. Behind the scenes, the former PM did his best to explain everything. Friends begged him to go public to set the record straight and tell his side of the story. He never did. Eventually they found out why. Mr. Mulroney hadn't been telling them the entire truth.

The cash payment was delivered in three parts, over a long period of time. Mr. Mulroney left the impression with friends that there was only one payment. Nor did he declare the money to the taxman until several years later. The excuse he eventually offered for the delay—that his life was in upheaval because of the RCMP investigation into the Airbus affair, in which the Mounties suspected he might be involved—makes no sense, because he got the money long before he ever heard of the investigation.

Then came new allegations that he was desperate to keep the payments secret. In a private conversation he had with William Kaplan, the author of a highly sympathetic book about him, he said: "Anyone who says anything about that will be in for one fuck of a fight." After that, Mr. Kaplan changed his mind, and wrote another book that portrayed Mr. Mulroney in a far less flattering light. What was the money for? That mystery has never been resolved.

A lot of folks relished the delicious thought of Mr. Mulroney going to jail for taking bribes. They figured that since Karlheinz Schreiber was handing out bags of cash as a lobbyist for Airbus, and Airbus planes were acquired by Air Canada on Mr. Mulroney's watch, and Mr. Mulroney took cash from him, then he must be guilty. But the dots never did connect. "It's inconceivable to me that Mulroney took a bribe in connection with Air Canada's purchase of the Airbus planes," Mr. Kaplan told me. "But that still doesn't answer the question of what the money was for and why he didn't declare it in the years he received it."

Everybody in politics knew that Schreiber stank. When Peter Lougheed ran Alberta, and Schreiber was trying to do land deals, Lougheed warned his cabinet to have nothing to do with him. John Crosbie, who was a senior minister under Mulroney, said he made sure to stay away from Schreiber at all times. "He was everywhere, he was ever-present. I had made my own decision to have nothing to do with him." Paul Tellier, who served as the country's top civil servant under Mr. Mulroney, heartily disliked the man and once threw him out of his office.

Back in the '90s, Mr. Mulroney was no doubt well aware of Mr. Schreiber's generous contributions to the party. In return, Mr. Schreiber was invited for breakfast at 24 Sussex and had unusual access to powerful people in Ottawa. Unlike Peter Lougheed, Mr. Mulroney never shut him down. The moment he was out of office, he gratefully accepted Mr. Schreiber's cash. He stashed the bills in various safety deposit boxes for six years, at which point Mr. Schreiber was indicted for fraud and bribery in Germany, and Mr. Mulroney decided it was prudent to declare the whole amount as income and make his peace with the taxman.

It's impossible to believe that such a shrewd and seasoned

politician was such a lousy judge of character. What's more likely is that he was a lousy judge of consequences. He thought the payments would never come to light. And so, for many years, Mr. Mulroney neglected to share the embarrassing details with his friends, even as they commiserated with him over his persecution at the hands of the Chrétienites, the Mounties, the CBC, Stevie Cameron and *The Globe and Mail*. He concealed his relationship with Schreiber until it was exposed by the media, and didn't bother to explain himself until long after he should have come clean.

In private, Mr. Mulroney continued to portray himself as the victim of an outrageous vendetta. In public, he decided the best defence was a good offence. During the keynote speech he gave at a fundraiser for his alma mater, St. Francis Xavier University, he stood tall with righteous anger. "I want to tell you tonight that I, Martin Brian Mulroney, eighteenth prime minister of Canada, will be there before the inquiry with bells on because I've done nothing wrong and I've got absolutely nothing to hide."

As for that cash—well, for someone with absolutely nothing to hide, Mr. Mulroney went to an awful lot of trouble to hide it. On the CBC's *the fifth estate,* Schreiber characterized the $300,000 (or $225,000) he handed over as a "deposit loan," which may have been something like the truth.

At the public inquiry called to investigate the Schreiber affair, Mulroney described the money as a retainer in return for acting as a high-level international door-opener (a common line of work for former top politicians). Mr. Schreiber groused that Mr. Mulroney barely did anything for his money. But Mr. Mulroney waxed poetic about his belief that Mr. Schreiber's military vehicles would enhance world peace. He was hopeful that once Bill Gates heard about Mr. Schreiber's pasta machine, he would be inspired to launch a global campaign against obesity (although the connection between the pasta machine and fat people was not entirely clear to me). In any event, he made it plain that he was no common shill. He was a statesman, and he worked hard for his money. He even subsidized this work from his own pocket, once he had decided it was prudent not to claim any of the $225,000, or however much he got, as expense money. In fact, Mr. Mulroney left the impression that, far from being on the take, he should be nominated for the Nobel Peace Prize.

Yet if a sizable percentage of Canadians remains convinced that Mulroney really was on the take, he can no longer blame his enemies for that. His shifting version of events made Bill Clinton ("It depends on what the meaning of the word 'is' is") look like the soul of candour. And the whole business made Canadians feel faintly banana-republic-ish. Just imagine that a former president of the United States, a few days out of office, was caught accepting envelopes of cash from a shady character like Karlheinz Schreiber—a man who was well known for bribing European politicians. Not only that, but the former politician gave a statement to law enforcers, under oath, in which he said he scarcely knew the man with the envelopes. Mr. Mulroney later defended himself by saying that he had been asked about his relationship with Schreiber during his time in office only, not afterwards, and therefore he had been technically accurate.

When the Oliphant Inquiry began its hearings in May 2009, some people thought it was not possible for Brian Mulroney to inflict more damage on himself than he had already. They were wrong. Mr. Mulroney left the witness stand a diminished man. After six gruelling days of testimony, the bombast and the self-pity were gone. He was weary and subdued. Perhaps he realized that he had failed to defend the indefensible—why he took the money in the first place, and why he'd waited so long to pay taxes on it. The only rational explanation is the simplest one. He must have thought nobody would find out.

For many years, Mr. Mulroney has been blaming his enemies in politics and the media for trying to destroy him. This obsession has become the leitmotif of his life. In his own mind, he is the victim— hounded and persecuted without mercy for imaginary crimes. I feel sorry for him.

But he was morally obliged to tell the whole truth, and he did not. It's sad to see such a gifted man so humiliated. But he humiliated his country too.

In an interesting twist, Brian Mulroney's appearance at the Oliphant Inquiry was briefly pushed out of the headlines by Conrad Black. People were stunned when the U.S. Supreme Court said it would review his conviction on some of the charges. Had Conrad's luck finally changed? Would he be exonerated at last?

Not entirely. The obstruction of justice conviction, which isn't being reviewed, could still keep him in jail for years. But his conviction on the fraud charges—which rests on a highly controversial interpretation of the law—stands a good chance of being overturned.

Later that same week in May, a stirring defence of Brian Mulroney by Conrad Black appeared in the *National Post*. "It is scandalous that Brian Mulroney is still being harassed over these accusations, seventeen years after leaving office," thundered Lord Black. "He rendered the country distinct service. Let us stop this foolishness and leave the man alone." It was one of the few voices raised in defence of Mr. Mulroney. He no doubt appreciated it—and doubtless wished that it had come from someone else.

Of the two disgraced men, Conrad Black may stand a better chance of redeeming himself in the court of public opinion. Although his business empire is gone for good, he still wields a formidable pen. As soon as the Supreme Court rules, he plans to unleash his scorching indictment of the entire U.S. justice system, which, he'll argue, used the mighty power of the state to pillory an innocent man.

Brian Mulroney was one of our better prime ministers. He engineered a historic free trade deal and pushed through an important tax reform that was widely reviled at the time, but ultimately embraced by his opponents. The verdict of historians on his place in history will probably be far kinder than the verdict of the public today. But he'll have to wait for it.

Conrad Black doesn't really care what other people think of him, because he knows he's always right. Brian Mulroney cares deeply what everybody thinks of him, and is tormented by the harm he's done to his own reputation.

One man is in jail. But my guess is that the other finds his punishment far harder to bear.

Chapter Four

Men on Top

A couple of years ago, my husband and I went to a family reunion in North Carolina. The highlight of the trip (for him) was a crummy little takeout shack called The Pigman. The Pigman made the best barbecue he'd ever tasted in his life.

Shortly after we returned home, a giant cargo truck lumbered up the driveway. Inside was a humongous dome-shaped apparatus that came all the way from Georgia. It was the barbecue of my husband's dreams. He was determined to give The Pigman a run for his money.

What is it with men and barbecues? My husband doesn't cook, except under duress. When I ask him to take care of dinner, he gets takeout curry or Swiss Chalet. But barbecuing stirs something primal in him. Cooking over open flame triggers some deep genetic memory in men of bringing home a chunk of bloody mastodon to toss on the fire. Women can never experience this thrill because we're just gatherers.

The new barbecue is no wimpy Weber. It is a Grill Dome, which, according to my husband, is the most superior barbecue technology available today. It can cook anything. It grills and smokes. It is not gas. It uses real charcoal lumps, not briquettes. The dome is made of a secret ceramic composition modelled after an ancient Japanese *kamado*. Best of all, you can fire it up to blast-furnace temperatures in mere minutes.

Our Grill Dome is large and black and egg-shaped, and weighs almost two hundred pounds. It now dominates our deck, like a household god that commands obeisance. "I haven't simply acquired a barbecue," my husband said. "I've opened the door to a whole new world."

Like everything men do, barbecuing is a competitive quest for status. Our friend Bob was a little jealous, even though he's got a stackable smoker with two different levels. He claims it's the Sistine Chapel of smokers. His greatest triumph was the day he smoked a chicken, a duck, a brisket, a salmon fillet and a salmon trout, all at the same time, each with a different secret marinade. "I felt like Michelangelo," he says.

According to him, any man can grill. But it takes a real man to smoke. "You've got to have a smoker if you want to stand tall," says Bob, who stands five feet, six and a half inches.

My husband planned his first masterpiece in detail. No grilled steak for him. He was determined to smoke something. So he went to the local boutique butcher and bought the finest, plumpest, air-chilled free-range chicken he could find. Unfortunately, he left it in the car overnight and it got smelly, and we had to throw it out. So I ran to Foodland and got an emergency factory chicken. My husband popped it in a pot of brine and various secret ingredients to marinate, and hoped for the best. He was worried because Bob was coming over. Women are competitive about their cooking, but subtly. Our competition consists of offering each other helpful advice and tips. Men are naked about it. They insist on showing off their inside knowledge, their exotic ingredients and their special expertise.

We have another friend, named Tom. When my husband bragged about his Grill Dome, Tom started telling us about his special secret rub, which he has been perfecting for the past twenty years. He makes it from sixteen different kinds of chili peppers he imports from Mexico. If you rub it all over a chicken and wrap the chicken in Saran Wrap and refrigerate it for three days, and then smoke it Tom's special way, you'll have the most sublime chicken you ever ate. Did I mention that Tom makes his own charcoal?

Women think barbecuing is a lesser form of cooking. Men think it's a high art. Take chips. "You have to decide whether you're going to use hickory, maple or mesquite," says Bob. "This isn't like deciding which bank you should get your mortgage at. This is life-changing." Right now, he's pondering whether he should try beechwood chips. Entire discussion forums on the Internet are devoted to these arcane matters. Can you use fruit pits or nutshells to produce smoke? Why does the membrane on back ribs come in different thicknesses? Many men are intensely focused on these things. Maybe it's what they do when they outgrow porn.

Another thing men like about barbecuing is all the special tools. To celebrate the arrival of the Grill Dome, I got my husband a new barbecue set at Williams–Sonoma. The implements come in a fake red leather box that's three feet long, and their handles all have leather thongs. The knife is the size of a samurai sword. The tongs could hoist a mastodon leg. He's thrilled.

But his first chicken was touch and go. To control the temperature on the Grill Dome, you have to wiggle the opening at the top and the notch at the bottom until the air flow is just right. This takes practice. The grill wasn't heating up fast enough, and Bob was coming over any minute. So my husband got my hair dryer and hooked it up to a very long extension cord and blasted hot air into the notch at the bottom. It worked. He was overjoyed.

"Men are really frail and powerless," says Bob. "Having complete control over the draft and venting of a mechanical object is very empowering."

To my relief, the chicken turned out to be delicious. It was golden brown and toasty on the outside, and moist and melting on the inside. It had a lovely smoky, faintly sweet flavour. Everyone but Bob agreed it was the best chicken they'd ever tasted. It was every bit as good as The Pigman's chicken, maybe even better. My husband was triumphant.

As we drifted off to sleep that night, I asked him how he'd done it. He confessed that he had ripped off his friend Bob's special super-duper secret ingredient and added it to the pot of brine the chicken had soaked in. He said he'd tell me what it was if I swore never to tell a soul. I swore.

"It was Coke," he said. "I used two cans of Coke."

Why do men still rule the world?

When I was a kid, life was simple. A girl could grow up to be a nurse, a teacher, a secretary or a ballerina. I chose ballerina. Unfortunately, I didn't have the talent. I was also built like a hearty German peasant. So I decided I would probably be a teacher instead.

Today, girls grow up to do everything. They're just as talented as boys, maybe more so. So why do men still rule the world? Why are almost all of the world's presidents, prime ministers, politicians, entrepreneurs and major CEOs still men, even in the liberated West? Should we still blame the glass ceiling and the old boys' club? Is there some kind of lingering, mysterious, systemic bias against women? Is the patriarchy still trying to keep us down?

As time goes by—and as women increasingly dominate fields that used to belong to men—these explanations explain less and less. It's time to look for other ones. One theory is something called the "jerk gene." Brain scans done on men show that they are genetically wired to win at all costs. Nothing makes them happier than beating out a rival, even when they know they have an unfair advantage. Because men are ultra-competitive, they're predisposed to behave like jerks (and also, let's face it, like heroes).

In his remarkable novel *Saturday,* Ian McEwan describes a friendly squash match that suddenly escalates into a vicious fight to the finish. It's a brilliant depiction of competitive male psychology, when reason vanishes and the world narrows to a single, overwhelming imperative: I've got to beat that bastard. Women are competitive, too. But few of us are as competitive as that. We also believe in playing fair, and we're less likely to behave like jerks. Our ambition generally does not involve the urge to win at any cost, or to beat our rivals to a pulp. Men tend to live by the immortal words of Vince Lombardi: "Winning isn't everything, it's the only thing."

Without sinking into gender essentialism, I think it's plain that men are drawn to dominance hierarchies. They pour a pile of energy and ambition into getting to the top. They'll pay a heavy price to gain and preserve their status (and will also be richly rewarded if they succeed). That's why recessions are harder on men. When a man loses his job he tends to experience it as a catastrophe—a serious loss of status. This kind of power matters less to women. I've known dozens of super-smart women who worked their butts off and rose through the ranks to become executive VP of something or other—only to say to hell with it when they no longer felt engaged or challenged, or when some jerk became their boss.

"Maybe the differences between the genders are more about motivation than ability," says social psychologist Roy F. Baumeister. That's one argument he makes in a brilliantly provocative essay called "Is There Anything Good About Men?" Professor Baumeister points out that there are far more men at both extremes of achievement—more CEOs, inventors and presidents, but also more criminals, junkies, suicides and losers. It's men who also do the dirty work (such as soldiering and coal mining). Human culture, he argues, "needs people to do dangerous or risky things, and so it offers big rewards to motivate people to take those risks. Most cultures have tended to use men for these high-risk, high-payoff slots. Some men reap big rewards, and others flop, fail and even die. Most shield their women from risks and also don't give them big rewards."

Why should this be so? Blame reproduction. Women are the ones who have the babies, so we're less expendable. Men are a dime a dozen. You can send them off to fight, explore and sail across the world in tiny boats because, reproductively speaking, a lot of them are surplus to requirements. The ones who do come back are heroes, move to the top of society and have lots of offspring. But for women, taking chances would be stupid, reproductively. We're better off to go along with the crowd and be nice. In other words, most of the human race is descended from men who took risks—and won—and women who played it safe.

Each gender has certain advantages over the other, but each advantage is linked to a disadvantage. This world of trade-offs adds up to something that Professor Baumeister calls a radical theory of gender equality. He writes, "Natural selection will preserve innate differences between men and women so long as the different traits are beneficial in different circumstances or for different tasks." For evolutionary reasons, he argues, men have larger networks of shallower relationships, while women have smaller networks of deeper relationships. "Men are much more interested than women in forming large groups and working in them and rising to the top in them." (And in beating large rival groups.) Think team sports, politics or large corporations. It's not that women can't excel at these endeavours. Of course we can. It's just that we don't care as much about them as men do.

There's more—about the cultural demands on men to earn respect, stand out from the herd, produce more than they consume and so on. Men are probably more driven to achieve, no matter what the cost. What might this mean in the world of science? "If you had any evolutionary understanding, you'd understand why there are more men in science," says Dr. Helena Cronin, an evolutionary theorist at the London School of Economics. "It's all about math proficiency. The heavier the math content, the heavier the distribution of males," she says, adding, "There's been all kinds of wriggling and writhing to explain this, and much policy to try to amend it." Even when we're science geniuses, many women prefer to do something that involves interacting with other people.

But the idea of difference is highly threatening. We conflate difference with inequality, fairness with sameness. We throw millions of dollars at schemes to recruit more women into science or detect deeply hidden biases against them. Instead, Dr. Cronin says, we should be devising teaching methods that take account of brain differences and help girls realize their maximum math potential. Not surprisingly, feminists tend to loathe Dr. Cronin (who calls herself a feminist Darwinist). But the facts don't care whether you like them.

If Professor Baumeister is right, it means that in spite of women's equal brains and spectacular achievements, men will keep winning most of the Nobel Prizes in math and physics. "More Nobels but also more dumbbells," adds Dr. Cronin. "I used to think that these patterns of sex differences resulted mainly from average differences between men and women in innate talents, tastes and temperaments. But among males, the variance—the difference between the most and the least, the best and the worst—can be vast. So males are almost bound to be overrepresented both at the bottom and at the top."

Why a good man is still hard to find

When I was thirty-something and still single, my girlfriends and I would get together over a glass of wine or three and bemoan the disastrous shortage of available men. All the good ones were taken, and half of the rest were gay. That left the dregs—men with drug habits, men who were happy being bicycle couriers and men with hygiene issues—to say nothing of men who were incurably commitment-phobic. There was no justice in the world. We were lively, attractive, successful and hankering to settle down. And we were sellers in a market that was beginning to feel like a sub-prime meltdown.

What's changed since then? Not much, according to the current generation of thirty-something single women. If anything, things have got worse. While women are busy buying condos and starting RRSPs, an alarmingly large number of men are busy swilling beer and playing Halo 3. Known as "slacker dudes," they've become a recognizable type in a host of movies (*Knocked Up*, *Pineapple Express* and the like) that have provided Canadian actor Seth Rogen with steady work.

Young men have always had to be roped and corralled into adult life. But they are refusing the bit as never before. Back in 1970, 69 percent of white men were married by the age of twenty-five, and 85 percent were married by the age of thirty. By 2000, the numbers had shrunk to 33 percent and 58 percent, respectively.

"For whatever reason, adolescence appears to be the young man's default state," writes social critic Kay Hymowitz in "Child-Man in the Promised Land," published in the February 2008 issue of *City Journal*. "It is marriage and children that turn boys into men," she claims. "Now that the single young man can put off family into the hazily distant future, he can—and will—try to stay a child-man."

In other words, why grow up, when you can get sex whenever you want and spend twenty-five hours a week playing with your Xbox 360?

Ms. Hymowitz has raised the hackles of men everywhere. To many of them, her argument sounds like a variation of the same "why men are evil" rants they've been enduring for the past thirty-five years. Others point out that marriage is hardly the deal that it used to be. Once upon a time, a husband could at least count on getting his socks washed. Now, marriage only guarantees that his domestic burdens will increase while his sexual choices will decrease.

It's not that women are entirely blameless either. One reason the good men are all taken is that when they were begging us to go out with them, we wouldn't give them the time of day. We were only interested in guys who were older, richer and more exciting, and so they married someone else. Then we got older ourselves and discovered that older, richer guys are only interested in women who are the age we used to be.

We also cling for far too long to our ridiculously delusional expectations. We want a man who's smart, handsome, romantic, monogamous, successful, taller than us and picks up his socks. Hah. We'd have better luck finding a nice Vancouver bungalow with a view for under half a million (even in today's real-estate market.)

If you suspect you may be among these deluded women, here's a hint: There is no Mr. Right. But there is probably a Mr. Not-So-Wrong with long-term growth potential. Millions of women have found happiness by broadening their search terms. And millions of men have found that it's not all that bad to grow up. Just don't expect him to give up his Xbox.

The passing of working-class masculinity

When the General Motors plant in Oshawa shut down for good this past spring, people wept. "It was a beautiful life," said Sue Stewart, whose husband, Bill, had spent thirty-one years working at GM. Bill wore a T-shirt that said: *Pride and Dignity—The Last Truck Rolls Off the Line.*

No matter what you think of the auto industry, the poignancy of these scenes is undeniable. It's the end of an era, not just for Sue and Bill, but for an entire way of life, when a man with a high-school education could raise a family, have a house with a backyard pool, and buy his-and-hers motorcycles so he could tool around the countryside with his wife on weekends. Bill is not to blame for what has happened to him. He's simply been flattened by history.

We're also witnessing the passing of something even more profound—a culture of working-class masculinity that has become an anachronism in the modern world. I have a dim memory of this culture. It flourished in the shop at the back of my father's heating and air-conditioning business back in the 1950s. The shop was behind the office, and it was where the real work got done. It was dark and noisy. There were girlie calendars. There were uncouth guys who yelled and smoked and swore and used bad grammar. They wore dirty coveralls, told filthy jokes, and reflexively disliked the boss. They were not very good at customer relations.

A lot of us would say: good riddance. Working-class culture was sexist, homophobic, casually racist and exclusively male. Not even auto plants are like that any more. At Ford's state-of-the-art plant in Brazil, half the workers are young women. The muscle work is done by robots. Everyone is flexible and works in teams, and the emphasis is on good communication. No one in my dad's shop would be remotely qualified to work there.

As low- and semi-skilled manual jobs disappear, working-class men are getting hammered—and so is their masculinity. "Manual labour has been a key source of identity, pride, self-esteem and power for working-class men," says a recent British study, which set out to probe a fascinating question: What makes these men so unemployable?

The conventional answer is that their education levels are too low and their skills are too poor. But the more accurate answer is that they're psychologically mismatched to the seismic shifts in our economy. The new economy (over the long term) is creating tons of service jobs in retail, customer support and personal care. The trouble is that these jobs require temperamental attributes that are stereotypically feminine—things like patience, a pleasant demeanour, deference to the customer and the ability to empathize and connect. Another way to put it is that these jobs require emotional labour, not manual labour. And women, even unskilled women, are much better at emotional labour than men are.

The author of the study, Darren Nixon, did his fieldwork in Manchester, where he interviewed dozens of long-term unemployed men. Once the embodiment of proud working-class culture, Manchester has had its guts ripped out by de-industrialization, and is trying to reinvent itself through the arts and tourism. Some of the men he interviewed had tried their hand at retail or other service jobs, but none had lasted long. "I've got no patience with people, basically," one subject told him. "I can't put a smiley face on." Or: "Telephone sales, no. Too much talking." Another man said, "If someone [a customer] gave me loads of hassle, I'd end up lamping [hitting] them." Several of them, in fact, had lost their jobs when they lamped the boss.

"Responding to the demands of customer sovereignty unquestionably is antithetical to young working-class men whose culture valorizes sticking up for yourself," writes the author in awkward academese. But his point is clear. The defining value of working-class masculinity is the ability to stick up for yourself when someone tries to give you shit. The defining requirement of service work (in their view) is having to eat it. Service work is a fundamental challenge to their masculine identity.

There used to be a lot of room in the world for men with muscle who didn't relate all that well to books or people. There was lots of dangerous and dirty work to do. They were the men who manned the ships, fished the seas, chopped down the trees and supplied the cannon fodder for countless wars. They mined the coal and made the trucks and bashed the metal in the mills.

They worked exclusively alongside other men in jobs that did not require them to put on a social mask, and did not call for aptitude in managing their emotions.

This identification of masculinity with hard physical work (no empathy required) is deeply embedded in the history of the human race. For eons, it has been the most common way to be a man. People are pretty adaptable, and education can work wonders. But no matter how much education and retraining we offer, we are not going to transform factory workers and high-school dropouts into customer-care representatives or nurses' aides anytime soon. It's their wives and daughters who will get those jobs. And in a world where even trash hauling has become tightly service-oriented (check out 1–800-GOT-JUNK?), many of these men will be permanently stranded.

In the new world of work, the old values of working-class men are out of date. And what we are really asking of them is not to retrain or upgrade. We are asking them to abandon their very idea of masculinity itself.

Chapter Five

Women and Children First

Like every other phase of life we reached, the Boomers revolutionized child-rearing. We invested more resources in our precious offspring than any generation in history—probably because we chose to have fewer of them. We resoundingly rejected older versions of child-rearing for being too rigid, too disciplined, too distant and too sexist. We imagined (with high anxiety) that our children were infinitely malleable little blank slates, who might achieve greatness with the right creative influences, or be ruined for the lack of them.

The biggest revolution has been in fathering. Most men today are more nurturing and more involved with their kids than their own fathers ever were. And many women have figured out how to juggle family and careers with immense resourcefulness.

On the whole, the kids have turned out wonderfully. But several astonishing and utterly unforeseen trends have emerged whose consequences we haven't quite begun to grasp. One is the triumph of young women in the academic sphere. Only fifteen years ago, people were still warning that girls suffered from subtle discrimination in the classroom. Today, girls rule—and it's the boys who are being left behind. Another development is the extension of adolescence well into our children's third decade—an age when previous generations had already become full-fledged adults. But the most startling development of all is the plummeting birth rate—a direct consequence of our success in creating equal opportunities for women.

When I get together with my female friends, for example, we don't talk much about our children. That's because half of us don't have any. We are a typical group of highly educated Boomer women—a lawyer, a PR consultant, a couple of entrepreneurs, a magazine editor and a judge. We've always got lots to talk about. But what's missing from our resumés is motherhood.

Why didn't we have children? We're not really sure. We had interesting jobs. We liked our independence. We never did see ourselves as happy-housewife types. It was never the right time. We were worried we wouldn't measure up. Our husbands (if we had them) weren't all that eager to be fathers. It seemed like too big a sacrifice. Children are expensive, and they demand a huge investment of parental energy. We also correctly guessed that long stretches of motherhood are tedious and dull.

So much for maternal instinct. When women have lots of options, the mothering instinct can get pretty weak. That's the way it's shaping up across the developed world. The higher the education and the income, the fewer the babies. Canada's fertility rate is holding steady at 1.5 children per woman. That's way below the replacement rate of 2.1. And there is no sign that our daughters, if we have any, will be any more reproductive than we were.

The mommy strike will profoundly transform the developed world, including Canada. If we can't replace ourselves, the country will shrink and grow poorer. That's one reason we need immigrants (although even doubling the immigration rate wouldn't be enough to replace the babies we're not having). Because we aren't having babies, Anglo-Saxon Canada will slowly dwindle away before our eyes, especially in the cities.

Immigrants are now a near-majority in Toronto, and before long, most Torontonians will be visible minorities. Newfoundland, Saskatchewan and the rest of rural Canada are emptying out. Moose Jaw and Carbonear are destined to be ghost towns, unless we can persuade Chinese and South Asian newcomers to settle there, which I doubt. Your *caffe latte*–coloured great-grandchildren (if you are lucky enough to have any) will be amazed to learn that people once lived in these remote spots, and that Canada was once overwhelmingly white.

We're fortunate compared to Europe or Japan, where fertility rates have crashed. By 2050, Europe will account for only 7 percent of the world's population. The United States, as usual, is the exception to the rule, mainly because of the huge influx of Hispanics.

Cultural conservatives blame the birth dearth on the loss of values in our secular, postmodern culture. Why have kids if people live only for themselves, nobody believes in sacrifice, and life is meaningless? The West has lost its way, and we're committing cultural suicide. That's the argument of the cultural critics. This theory is not without appeal, but things aren't that simple. Fertility rates have also plunged below replacement levels throughout South America and East Asia, including poor nations such as Vietnam and Myanmar (Burma). They are now below replacement in Algeria, Tunisia, Lebanon and Iran. They are even below replacement in Calcutta,

Mumbai and New Delhi. (New Delhi was the city that inspired Paul Ehrlich to write *The Population Bomb,* the wildly popular book that predicted mass starvation was right around the corner.) More than half the world's population may now live in countries with "sub-replacement" fertility.

The mommy strike has driven the demographers (most of whom are men, need I add) around the bend. They were sure that birth rates would never fall below replacement levels. They were wrong. Then they assumed that the mommy strike would strike only rich, developed nations like ours. Wrong again. It turns out that poor people who can get their hands on birth control want smaller families too.

So why aren't women having babies? Aren't we hard-wired to want kids? The answer seems to be, it depends. If you're an illiterate peasant, children are an asset. They provide free labour. They are also your old-age insurance, because they will probably feed you when you're old and useless. But when society becomes literate, children become an expense, because you've got to educate them if you want them to succeed. And, in more developed nations, the state will feed you when you're old and useless.

As soon as women become highly educated income-earners, the cost of having children becomes staggeringly high. For upper-middle-income families, the financial disincentives are so great that it's amazing professional women have any children at all. "No society until recent times has expected love alone to support the family enterprise," writes the economist Shirley Burggraf (a woman, you may note). "To put it another way, parental love has never cost so much."

Throughout the developed world, politicians are desperately offering bribes to defray the high cost of parental love. In Russia—

where the population is in free fall and the most endangered species is the Russian—Vladimir Putin offered a bonus of $10,000—a
stupendous amount—to any parents who have a second child,
plus monthly subsidies and better-paid maternity leaves. In Japan,
another doomed nation, local municipalities are offering extra cash
in hopes that they won't vanish off the map. In Singapore, where
the fertility rate has dwindled to about one child per couple, parents get $3,000 for the first child, $9,000 in cash and savings for the
second, and up to $18,000 for each one after that.

Good luck to them. So far, there's no evidence that incentives
work—not family-friendly policies, or generous parental leaves, or
virtually free daycare for all (as in Quebec), or cold, hard cash. Perhaps one day we'll get so desperate that fertile young women will
be offered jobs for life as professional breeders, in return for anything they want. Or maybe we'll just start test-tube farms. In the
meantime, give every mom you know a hug. Our country needs
them as never before.

————

Sooner or later, most mothers are going to need someone to look
after the kids. And daycare (or childcare, as it's now often called)
is one issue that has generated more nonsense and more hysteria
than almost any other subject I have tackled in my columns. The
daycare lobby has been clamouring for heavily subsidized universal
daycare for years. It would cost Canada at least ten billion dollars a
year, but, after all, they argue, our children's future is at stake.

How could anyone be against universal daycare? It's like being
against kids. But the daycare discussion is full of emotional manip-
ulation, misdirection and built-in stupidities. The daycare alarmists
make no distinction between state-paid daycare for poor kids and

state-paid daycare for children of the lawyer couple up the street. Look at France, they say. France has free daycare for everyone! France also has private, two-tier medicine, but I don't see any backers of universal daycare advocating that.

Daycare in Quebec costs parents just seven dollars a day, no matter how well off they are. Interestingly, this program was not launched because children were perceived to be falling between the cracks. It was launched because a former premier, Lucien Bouchard, wanted to encourage Quebec women, who have the lowest birth rate in Canada, to have more babies (presumably francophone ones). It didn't work. The women of Quebec refused to do their duty to the state. But they and their spouses did rush to get something for almost nothing, and the demand for seven-dollar daycare rapidly outstripped supply. Today, the program's cost has soared into the billions. It threw the province deeply into hock, but when the current premier, Jean Charest, tried to cut it back, he found it was politically untouchable.

Quebec's program is a massive middle-class entitlement that helps the haves but not the have-nots. Most of the children who use it are from upper-income families. It discriminates against parents who stay home to raise the kids themselves. Poor families, the ones who ought to benefit the most, tend not to use the program at all.

The daycare industry would have you believe that, without appropriate stimulation at the proper developmental stages by licensed professionals, most children will grow up to be morons. This is nonsense. Dozens of studies have found that most kids will turn out fine no matter who takes care of them. Cheap, convenient and informal daycare does nothing to harm kids, but it does do quite a bit to ease the lot of harried parents. As I drive to work through my pleasant downtown neighbourhood, I see the victims of unregulated daycare everywhere. They are being wheeled through the park by untrained babysitters, or foreign-looking nannies, or (horrors) by the mom who lives next door. There are even kids with men (who appear to be their dads). I suspect that not one of those adults is a qualified early childhood education instructor. The kids don't look as if they're suffering, but what do I know? I'm just an amateur. Child-care experts say parents and other uninformed adults are not capable of distinguishing between high-quality daycare and all the other kinds. That's why we need experts.

But it's not these children of the middle class whose future really is at stake. The real daycare crisis concerns the thousands and thousands of kids who actually need professional help—typically children of struggling, poorly educated single mothers who can't give them the support and stimulus they need. And that's the tragedy of the daycare wars, because in a world of limited resources, they're the biggest losers.

There's an even greater heresy in the daycare wars. It's the claim that a very young child is much better off at home with her mommy. In spite of what the experts say, most mothers instinctively know this. And most parents in Quebec know Jean-François Chicoine. His regular media appearances have made him the most famous pediatrician in the province. *Le bon Dr. Chicoine,* as they call him, is the baby doctor people trust.

But then, this personable young pediatrician unleashed a bomb-shell—a 520-page indictment of social practices that he believes are harmful to our kids. His most explosive charge: too many parents parachute their kids into daycare at far too young an age. His book is called *Le bébé et l'eau du bain* (*The Baby and the Bathwater*). "In Quebec," he writes, "children are kept in daycare fifty-two weeks a year, for about sixty hours a week. . . . Children learn to say the word 'mommy' without being cuddled by their mother, and nobody seems bothered by that."

Challenging daycare in Quebec is like challenging a way of life. Universal daycare is a cornerstone of social policy. There are more than 50,000 children in care under the age of two, and almost every neighbourhood boasts a *centre de la petite enfance*. Daycare activists are deeply worried that people like Dr. Chicoine might whip up a backlash that will undermine the case for public daycare and drive mothers back into the home.

Dr. Chicoine insists he's not political. He has only one agenda: kids. And he ardently believes that the best place for most kids under two is with their parents. "At this time of life, it is very important for the baby to get a lot of affection and form a sense of security," he told me. "That is the basis for intelligence, future behaviour and a lot of other things."

His conclusions are based on a large body of recent research about attachment theory, as well as twenty years of personal observation. "Between birth and eight months, the child will attach to the world, and the mother or father will attach to their baby," he says. Those eight months are just as crucial for the parent as for the baby. Forget maternal instinct. Parents need time, he says, to "fall in love."

Between eight and fifteen months, the baby will gradually be able to trust people other than the primary caregiver—but five at the most. Now look at daycare. "In daycare, a baby will encounter an average of seventeen different caregivers between those ages," says Dr. Chicoine. "During the summer, it's five or six a day." For a child so young, having to deal with so many strangers can be an unsettling, even terrifying, experience.

Sleep problems, feeding problems and behaviour problems are typical short-term results of attachment disorder. But Dr. Chicoine is convinced the consequences can be more serious and long-lasting. Children may develop learning disorders and have difficulties in school. They may turn into troubled adolescents. Their ability to trust their parents may be permanently impaired. Not all children will suffer all these adverse effects. In fact, most won't. If they have good parents, chances are they'll be fine. But a significant minority—one in four, at a rough guess—"will be lost."

Dr. Chicoine believes that daycare is worst for families who need it the most—the blue-collar families who work long hours and struggle to get by on two meagre incomes. The mother has no choice but to go back to work quickly, usually to a menial job she doesn't like. Her child spends long hours in care that is often "mediocre, even pathetic"—and both mom and baby are constantly stressed out.

Dr. Chicoine argues that feminists have done these women a significant disservice. What they really need is not full-time daycare for their one-year-olds. What they need is a way to stay home. He sees a massive disconnect between feminist daycare advocates—who tend to be highly educated career women—and your average high-school-graduate mom, who has a job, not a career, and works because she must. "These women are getting screwed by having to return to work too early," he says bluntly.

Attachment theory isn't popular among daycare advocates because it raises extremely uncomfortable questions about the compatibility (or not) of careers and motherhood. Today, when you have a baby, you're supposed to tell the world that nothing's changed. You're supposed to pretend that you're just as productive and just as thin as before. You're supposed to get a breast pump and use it in the washroom between meetings. You spend a lot of energy pretending everything's the same. But if you put a baby into daycare at two months old, why have a baby at all? It's as if staying at home with your child were a punishment.

In case you think Dr. Chicoine hates daycare, he doesn't. In fact, he thinks we need to invest more money in it, especially to attract quality daycare workers. He believes that infant daycare—very high-quality infant daycare, unlike the kind on offer today—can be of real benefit to children from seriously deprived backgrounds. He also thinks daycare (in moderation) is fine for kids over two or two-and-a-half, who are old enough to benefit from the socialization it offers.

But he has tackled the taboo subjects of class and status, and the divergent interests of working-class and professional women. And he has loaded on the guilt. So how does he respond to the guilty mom (or dad) who reads his book, and can't figure out how she (or he) can possibly stay home for two whole years of a baby's life?

"If she asks the question, then we've succeeded," he says. "I want her to think. It's her right to think. I don't think it's a matter of fear or guilt. It's the beginning of responsibility."

Girls and boys together

Girls today have a poise and self-confidence that astonish me. They have a rock-solid feeling of equality that took my generation half a lifetime to achieve. Their sense of themselves has changed profoundly since I was in school. Unlike us, they've grown up in a world where there is nothing women cannot do.

The girls I know are champion debaters and editors of their campus newspapers. They take home the medals at science fairs. They have no trouble speaking up among a group of boys and making themselves heard. They're destined to become top lawyers, doctors, judges, researchers and administrators in unprecedented numbers. If you thought the feminist revolution was over, think again. Its most profound effects are still to come.

Ontario's Trent University is proud of its undergraduate focus and small-town feel. On its homepage is a picture of a happy-looking Asian guy—a double-minority student. Maybe one reason he looks so happy is that he's got his pick of girls. Trent's gender ratio skews 60-to-40 female. That's typical for universities these days. In the liberal arts the ratio is two to one. Graduation rates are even more lopsided. At the University of Ottawa, the graduation rate for women is 88 percent, compared to the mid-50s for men.

"Women are consistently our strongest students in the faculty of arts and social sciences," said Neil Gold, provost of the University of Windsor. "It worries me a bit what's happening to the men." Women outnumber men in biology, chemistry, law and medicine. The only places males still rule are in physics and engineering.

This decisive superiority in educational achievement will never be mirrored perfectly in the workforce. Testosterone (a.k.a. the alpha male hormone) and the urge to nurture are the two reasons why. But the kinds of skills in demand in the Information Age give girls a huge leg up.

Should we be worried about what's happening to their brothers? Or is the famous "boy crisis" just a lot of hype? Sara Mead, the author of a 2006 book called *The Truth about Boys and Girls*, argues that most boys are doing better than ever. And if the girls are doing even better than the boys, so what? "While most of society has finally embraced the idea of equality for women, the idea that women might actually surpass men in some areas (even as they remain behind in others) seems hard for many people to swallow."

Ms. Mead's study made a giant splash. "Talk of the boy crisis is a diversion," wrote *New York Times* columnist Judith Warner. She blames the alleged crisis on overwrought upper-middle-class parents who push their kids too hard. The real trouble with their sons is emotional and behavioural, not academic. Besides, achievement gaps by race are bigger than achievement gaps by gender. The boy crisis is really a crisis of race and class.

The backlash was probably inevitable. The "boy crisis" has boosted a lot of careers and sold a lot of magazines, just as the "girl crisis" did in the '90s. "The 'boy crisis' offers an attractive way for conservative pundits to get in some knocks against feminism and progressive education," said Ms. Mead.

So what's the truth?

The truth is, boys have been lagging behind girls for many years, and the gap seems to be growing. Once upon a time, that didn't matter. Now it does. "Basically, boys are flatlined," says Judith Kleinfeld, director of the Boys Project at the University of Alaska. "They aren't keeping up with the demands of an economy that relies increasingly on highly technical skills." In one international test of literacy skills, fifteen-year-old girls in Canada outperformed fifteen-year-old boys by 30 percent. Among black kids, girls go on to post-secondary education at twice the rate of boys.

"Many boys, especially working-class boys, get caught in what I call 'the trap,'" Professor Kleinfeld says. "They take a high-paying job, maybe even $20 an hour, working the forklift at night at Walmart. Then they injure their backs, have a lot of debt and no skills to fall back on." But her research shows that boys of every background have fallen behind. Among the white sons of college-educated parents, reading skills have dropped dramatically. In one national achievement test, 23 percent of such boys scored "below basic" in reading and writing at the end of Grade Twelve (compared with 7 percent of the girls). This means they can't read a newspaper or simple instructions—and these are the well-off kids.

For a big minority of boys, high school is a hostile and unnatural place. It's a place where hormone-laced adolescents are required to sit for hours at a time without squirming, where compliance, neatness, rule-following and politeness are rewarded. It's a world that's mostly run by women. Men now make up the smallest percentage of teachers in the past forty years. Meantime, boys are supposed to pay attention while women drone on about subjects that have no relevance to their daily life. Good literature is anything by Toni Morrison. Normal male competitiveness is interpreted as deviance, and horseplay as sexual harassment. A sizable percentage of male inmates have been labelled "special ed." or "behavioural" (i.e., deficient) from an early age.

Is it any wonder so many boys think school is hell?

Consider all the ways we've turned normal boyhood into deviancy. My favourite photo of my brother shows him at around eight. He is outside, sitting on the curb—a scrawny, grubby, geeky-looking kid with a rip in his jeans and a scrape on his knee. His glasses are held together with duct tape. He had a terrible temper then. The story of how he finally beat up the local bully, the one who broke his glasses, is still the stuff of family legend. Today, a boy like my brother would be dosed with Ritalin. He'd never be allowed to ride his bike out to the forest preserve by himself, and certainly not without a helmet. He'd probably spend most of his summer indoors, playing video games, and getting anti-bullying counselling.

Has something essential been scrubbed from boyhood? A lot of people think so. That's why *The Dangerous Book for Boys* was such a monster hit. Written as a guide to the things that every boy should know, the book was a runaway best-seller.

"I wanted to celebrate boys," said the author, Conn Iggulden. The book explains such manly arts as how to make a water bomb, how to navigate without a compass, how to play Texas Hold 'Em, and how to hunt, kill, skin and cook a rabbit. It has tales of famous battles, physical courage and derring-do. It also says the most essential tool for any boy to have is a Swiss Army knife. Advice like that is what makes this book dangerous, I guess. When a friend of mine gave his twelve-year-old son a Swiss Army knife, the kid inadvertently went to school with it and was suspended for three days when it fell out of his pocket. Both father and son were treated like mass murderers in the making.

As we make the world an ever-safer place for children, we aren't always doing kids a favour. They need to skin their knees sometimes. "We picked up scrapes and bruises and we considered them badges of honour," says Mr. Iggulden. "It's an important learning experience." And if we don't allow boys to take risks, they'll take even worse risks on their own.

The other point he makes is that boys and girls are different. His book contains nothing about feelings or relationships but a lot about how to do stuff. "On the whole, boys are more interested in the use of urine as secret ink than girls are."

But the school system has been completely feminized. As tag and dodge ball are banned, and competition is banished in favour of co-operation, and group learning takes precedence over individual results, it's no wonder boys are losing out. The people who say we have a boy problem are right. But instead of trying to change boys, maybe it's time we tried to change the system.

It's our fault they can't grow up

Given the boy problem it's not surprising that "the boomerang generation"—young adults who still live at home—is predominantly male. A lot of friends of mine are worried that their twenty-something kids are stalled in life. Their basements are stashed with grown men (and women) with aspirations to be filmmakers and golf pros. I have other friends whose kids have finally moved out, but the parents refuse to sell the house in case the kids want to move back. Another friend of mine told me the other day she wants to take a week off to get her daughter settled into her new school. I was floored. The kid is twenty-three. She has an IQ in the stratosphere. She knows her way around much of the Third World, and her new school is Harvard Law.

The infantilization of our children has reached ridiculous extremes. It's now trite to say that thirty is the new twenty—the age at which true maturity begins. But it's not just the fault of overly indulgent parents. The whole culture is to blame. These are our trophy kids. We raised them to believe the world was theirs and they could do anything they wanted. We made sure they would never fail. They grew up playing sports where everyone gets a trophy just for showing up. Their teachers stopped using red ink to mark their tests because red ink might hurt their self-esteem.

We've been brainwashed to believe that succeeding in the Information Age demands more education (i.e., credentials) than ever before. These days, a BA is simply what a high-school diploma used to be. And a period of extended dependency is the price you've got to pay to become a functional adult in the Information Age.

But is the price too high? Maybe the postponement of adulthood is a spectacular waste of human potential. A lot of those twenty-somethings, trapped in the ever-longer twilight zone

73

between adolescence and adulthood, are aimless, frustrated, a little angry, and mildly depressed. They're not in control of their lives. Instead of plunging into the world of productive work, they spend years piling up more "credentials" as they try to figure out what they really want to do and wait for just the right self-actualizing opportunity to come along. As for credentials, it's true that some professions require years of academic training. But many others don't. Dozens of professions (such as journalism) have been "credentialized" without any noticeable improvement to the product.

It's shocking to recall how young the age of adulthood used to be. George Washington was bossing a survey team in Indian country when he was sixteen. Roman boys were marrying and joining Roman legions when they were fourteen. Unmarried girls were old maids at twenty-five. Many of the Pilgrims on the *Mayflower* were in their early twenties. None of them had eighteen years of schooling. But they had the fortitude, competence and judgment of full-fledged adults.

Psychologist Robert Epstein, the author of a book called *The Case Against Adolescence,* argues that we'd all be better off if we could let our kids grow up. In his provocative new book, he argues that extended adolescence is bad for everyone. The affliction known as adolescence is a recent historical development. Many pre-industrial cultures, where teenagers are integrated into adult life, don't even have a word for it. Adolescence exists only in Western industrial countries, where education and laws have isolated teenagers from adults. We all know the pathologies of adolescence—the awful conflicts between parents and children, the drugs and alcohol, the obsession with appearance, the negative peer pressure, the moods, depression and anger, the cheap material culture. It's a miserable stage of life.

The modern education system was created in order to supply the factories of the Industrial Age with a reliable stream of standardized, skilled labour. Today, the Industrial Age is dead, and the factory system is obsolete. The knowledge that people need for most jobs is specialized and changes quickly. But we still educate our kids in the same old way. "We need education spread over a lifetime, not jammed into the early years," he argues. "Past puberty, education needs to be combined in interesting and creative ways with work."

Yet we still insist that young adults, many of whom are indifferent and unmotivated, stay incarcerated in school until they're old enough to legally escape. Instead of admitting that this model doesn't work any more, our plan is to extend it until the poor kids turn eighteen.

And then they go to university. Our assumption is that universities should be for everyone. In the late 1960s, only 10 percent of high-school graduates went on to college or university. Today, it's about 40 percent—and the stampede shows no sign of letting up. In Canada, a million young adults are enrolled in full- or part-time post-secondary education. As a result, we're overeducating and miseducating quite a lot of people.

Our mistake is to imagine that universities have the power to transform average people into smart ones. Of course they don't. And universities are now accepting a lot of students who shouldn't really be there. Nobody, however, is about to tell them that, least of all their parents. Their professors won't tell them, either. Universities compete for bodies to fill the seats—that's the way they're funded by governments—and customer satisfaction is important. You can't flunk them just because they can't write. One faculty member I know who returned to teach English after a decade in administration was astounded at the students' decline in writing ability. He admitted that he should have failed most of them. But he didn't dare. University departments are rewarded for high enrolments, and you won't attract students if you fail them.

In *Ivory Tower Blues,* Jim Côté, a sociology professor at the University of Western Ontario, and co-author Anton Allahar argue that the usefulness of a BA (especially of the liberal arts variety) is vastly overrated. "You've got to distinguish between skills and credentials," they say. "And a liberal arts education is not job training unless you want to be a liberal arts professor."

Many students find this out the hard way. And so, after getting their BAs, they head off to community college to pick up yet another diploma in advertising or PR or media studies. The main effect of all this higher education is to prolong the period of adolescence and dependency. Whether it improves the workforce is open to debate. Instead of producing unskilled high-school graduates, we now produce unskilled university graduates, a generation of twenty-somethings trapped in the ever-expanding twilight zone between childhood and maturity.

"There's an epidemic of work unpreparedness," says Professor Côté. "It relates to being coddled and isolated from adult society. A lot of employers are complaining that new graduates aren't prepared to pay their dues and put in hard hours."

Don't blame them. Blame us, for keeping them helpless and dependent.

Robert Epstein has a radical proposal for the problem of extended adolescence: shorter compulsory school hours, mandatory education for basics only, more individualized instruction, and an end to age segregation. He'd also repeal the laws that restrict younger adults from doing adult jobs, owning property and all the rest. The idea that people have to be crammed full of knowledge for sixteen years before they're fit to enter the adult world needs a serious rethink. If they have a basic grasp of words and numbers, why can't they pick up job skills and extra education as they need them? Isn't that what lifelong learning is all about? And what's wrong with vocational schools for teenagers—common in many parts of Europe—that are obliged to coordinate their programs with local labour markets?

Mr. Epstein points out that we routinely underestimate what teenagers can do. "Some of them can barely read or write but all of them can get their driver's licence," he says. Our idea that the teenage brain is not fully developed is simply wrong. On competency and intelligence tests, teenagers score pretty much the same as adults. The reason they don't act like adults is because we don't treat them like adults. "We need to give young people incentives to join the adult world and move out of the insane, completely vacuous world of teen culture," he says. "Teens should be learning from the people they are about to become."

Of course this will never happen. Society—in the form of the vast education industry, as well as much of the entertainment and fashion industries—has far too much invested in keeping kids from growing up. Older workers have a certain interest in delaying the entry of younger, smarter, faster rivals into the labour market. And since the economy fell of a cliff, it's gotten a lot worse. Our kids always figured they'd land a good job, on their terms, with lots of flexibility and free time. If not, they could always stay in school for a while longer. After all, they'd have their parents to cushion them. They didn't bank on steep tuition hikes, or parents who'd lost half their savings. As for an inheritance one day, forget it. They'll be lucky to get help with the down payment on a six-hundred-square-foot condo.

What really worries me is that our kids are never going to forgive us. We gave them everything. We never told them life could be so unfair. We never told them our real legacy would be a pile of debt as high as Mount Everest. And twenty-five or thirty years from now, when the Boomers are sucking the last dollars from the health-care system, we shouldn't be surprised if they sneak in and turn off our ventilators. Would you blame them?

Chapter Six

The Busybody State Does Not Approve

In Toronto, public-health officials are worried that we're getting too much sun. In Halifax, they tried to pass a bylaw making it mandatory to put cats on leashes. In Montreal, they want to ban wood stoves. Lawn spray has been outlawed almost everywhere. As for garbage—don't get me started. No matter how hard I try, the waste police keep rejecting my garbage whenever I inadvertently break the rules. It used to be that our governments had important things to do—run the schools and hospitals, fix the potholes, and keep us safe. But now, it seems, they spend most of their time hounding us into virtue.

In my home city of Toronto, for example, the city government doesn't even trust grown-ups to choose their own lunch. Toronto is the only city in the world where street vendors have to pass an ethnically correct nutrition test. And believe me, this is progress. Until now, street food in Toronto was restricted to the lowly hot–dog cart. In a city with more ethnic restaurants than you could ever count, the most exotic street food you could get was pre-cooked sausage on a bun.

But then, a couple of years ago, our far-seeing city council resolved to change all that. Nothing to it, really. You just decide how many licences to issue, and make sure the vendors pass food-safety checks. At least that's how every other city does it. Not us. Here's how we do it. First, the city councillors decided to purchase a fleet of carts and lease them back to the vendors. When the cost ($700,000) proved too prohibitive, they specified an official city-approved cart, which vendors are required to buy for as much as $28,000, not including licences and location fees. (Why does a food cart cost more than a car? It's a mystery to me.)

Would-be vendors were required to submit their food plans, with samples. All submissions were graded on a long list of criteria, including food safety, nutrition, use of local food, business plan, eth-nic diversity, and home-cooked taste (even though all the food must be produced in commercial kitchens). A taste test was conducted by a four-chef judging panel. Hot dogs and sausages were strictly forbidden, because the city is only interested in "healthy options."

In the end, only eight plucky contestants made the grade. Many others were defeated by the high costs of entry and the red tape. For example, the owner of the cart must be on site at least 70 percent of the time (no conglomerates allowed here!), and any change of menu must be pre-approved by the Medical Officer of Health. Absent from the new offerings were such staples as hot pretzels, falafel, and the peameal bacon sandwich—Hogtown's signature delicacy.

In New York City, food diversity runs amok without the slight-est help from City Hall. Foodies can try corn-based patties from Colombia called *arepa de choclo,* or hot steamy Mexican tamales dripping with fatty pork and chile oil. How about some *halal,* which is dark-meat chicken with green sauce, or Chinese *cheung fun* with spongy curried fish balls and ultra-fatty pork skin? Then there are fried-fish sandwiches on Wonder Bread, and something best described as corn poutine, which consists of toasted corn kernels sautéed in lard and smothered with mayo, cheese and lime. It's revolting, but delicious.

New Yorkers are allowed to judge the street food for themselves. Naturally, we could never do this in Toronto, a city run by control freaks who think street food should be about social justice and nutritionism. And don't even mention bottled water. It's been banned from city premises because it's anti-environmental. From now on, thirsty citizens will just have to drink Coke.

Although I didn't know it at the time, I was blessed to be a youth during those fleeting years when nothing was forbidden and all things were permitted. We smoked. We drank. We had unprotected sex with strangers. We even drank water straight from the tap. The dark cloud of sexually transmitted disease was not yet on the horizon, and we never gave a thought to AIDS, second-hand smoke, sexual harassment, or our cholesterol. 'Twas bliss to be alive back then, and I pity all of you who weren't. My favourite line in poetry comes from William Blake: "Damn braces. Bless relaxes."

It's all braces now. The list of prohibitions on correct behaviour stretches further than the distance that those wretched smokers are now obliged by law to separate themselves from our office buildings, lest any wayward curl of deadly tobacco fumes contaminates the rest of us. No more sheltering from the icy blasts for them! Smokers have been banished from outdoor patios, too, even when they are well ventilated by the prevailing winds. Ontario and Nova Scotia now ban smoking in cars where a minor is present, and other provinces may follow suit. Recently in Ontario, a twenty-year-old was busted under this law. While the policeman was writing out a whopping $155 ticket for the driver, the fifteen-year-old girl (a minor) who was his passenger got out of the car and (quite legally) lit up a cigarette.

Personally, I detest cigarette smoke. I believe that everyone has an inalienable right not to be exposed to it against her will. The arrival of the smoke-free workplace was a triumph for human rights and simple common sense. But our creeping prohibitionism has long since crossed a line. Smoking bans are no longer about protecting non-smokers from the (highly exaggerated) dangers of second-hand smoke, although that is what we're told. They are really about punishing smokers. Instead of doing the honest thing and just banning smoking altogether, the state will simply harass and marginalize the deviants until they quit.

This strategy is thought to be cruel and unacceptable when applied to, say, panhandlers, heroin addicts and people who prefer marijuana. But we don't think panhandlers and heroin addicts are a menace to society. Smokers are. And so we're happy to forbid our wrinkled Second World War vets from sharing a smoke with their buddies at the Legion. Some people call that progress. I call it insufferable sanctimony.

Something has gone wrong when the busybody state can make an outlaw of Christopher Hitchens, the most entertaining public intellectual of our age. Mr. Hitchens was in Toronto a while ago, and packed a restaurant with his fans. He illicitly puffed his way through several dozen Rothmans Blues. People worried we might get busted.

Mr. Hitchens has a theory about the progressive intrusion of the busybody state. "I think it's a mingling of the Puritan and in some

ways the Catholic traditions. One is not allowed to let someone go
to hell in their own way, so it is a religious duty in effect to inter-
vene for their own good," he says. "It is overlaid now by the very
sanctimonious idea that, if you can mention health and especially
if you can get the word *kid* into the same sentence, you are entitled
to do anything. There is no privacy you can't invade."

Can the busybodies go any further? Of course they can! One
town in California (the cradle of the non-smoking movement) has
banned smoking altogether, except in the privacy of one's own
home. Nobody complained. And when the city fathers and mothers of Los Angeles passed a law banning more fast-food joints from
South L.A., they approved of that too.

Here in Canada, we love obeying rules. We're a nation of natural
compliers. Have you tried crossing against the light lately? People
shoot you glances that let you know you're doing something quite
transgressive, even when there's not a single car in sight. That's how
Mr. Hitchens must have felt.

Despite the smoking crisis, the obesity crisis and several other
lifestyle crises, people are living longer and are in better health
than ever. The real crisis (from the authorities' point of view) is that
they are running out of useful things to do. Doing useful things is
their raison d'être. And so they must get busy whipping up pan-
ics over increasingly marginal threats to public safety. They harass
smokers, ban bad dog breeds and plastic ducks, banish Roundup
weed spray, and wage campaigns against pop vending machines in
schools. They mount awareness campaigns against the hazards of
wearing scented deodorant in public.

And now they've found a really big one—the sun.

As we all know by now, too much sunlight is bad for you. This
may strike some folks as a funny thing for Canadians to worry

about, seeing that we don't get enough of it six months a year. But the City of Toronto has decided to worry about it anyway. The authorities figure that parents can't be trusted to limit their children's sun exposure to the appropriate amounts. So the bureaucrats will do it for them. Not even the most powerful bureaucrats can regulate the sun—yet—but they can, and will, regulate the shade. And so the city has dispatched workers to our playgrounds and other public spaces to conduct what are known as "shade audits."

These audits will measure the angle of the sun at different times of day, as well as the amount of direct and reflected sunlight, the quantity and usability of shade from trees and other structures, and how many children are likely to be in attendance. Then they will determine where our little ones are likely to be most at risk from dangerous UV rays that cause deadly skin cancer. I can guarantee it's not in my part of town, where conscientious parents cover their children with so much protective goop and gear that it's a wonder they don't come down with rickets.

But why take chances? As one city councillor argued, "It makes no sense to me that people would object to fighting an epidemic of skin cancers among children." Regrettably, not all children live in the leafier parts of town. So we have a special duty to protect the less fortunate children who live in high-rises, and are forced to play in hazardous sun-drenched public parks. Personally, I think we should be happy the little tykes are outside at all. What we really need is a public-health campaign to pry them from their video games. But provincial officials are so busy conjuring up imaginary dangers it's remarkable that parents ever let their kids out the door at all. Heat alert! Heat alert! Any day the mercury hits 32.1, they declare a heat alert. Where did these people grow up? Iqaluit?

The city's sprawling Shade Policy Committee (which includes

environmental planners, foresters, meteorologists, dermatologists, architects, parks personnel, oncologists and a "healthy lifestyles" nurse) is a bureaucrat's delight. It is the logical offshoot of a mindset that believes ordinary people are completely incapable of exercising common sense, combined with the belief that the right policies, devised by wise public officials like themselves, can save the world.

I have nothing against the shade. I even think it would be nice if the city had more of it. I just wonder why we need so many experts to figure out where to plant a tree.

Which brings me to the bane of my existence, garbage. If Canada had a state religion, it would be recycling. If you doubt this, ask your kids. They may not have picked up much reading, 'riting and 'rithmetic in school, but they all know the three r's that really count: reduce, reuse, recycle. So crucial is this virtue to our national identity that the word *recycling* receives a special mention in the government booklet that prepares immigrants for their citizenship test. It is listed among the most important English-language words they ought to know. They learn that if they want to be good citizens, they must recycle.

In Toronto, the biggest civic issue today is not the legions of homeless people sleeping on the sidewalk, our decrepit docklands, or the traffic gridlock that is strangling the city. It's garbage—how to sort it, divert it, minimize it and get rid of it, and the best ways to convert citizens to the cause. Once considered a perfectly normal by-product of civilization, garbage has become, in the modern mind, a symbol of all that is unwholesome, unclean and immoral. It is unclean in the spiritual sense, a daily reminder of mankind's fallen state. You can be sure that angels, if they exist, do not produce any garbage at all. Environmental purists say if we were better, we wouldn't either. The amount of garbage we produce is the precise measure of our mortal sin and error, and the more there is of it, the wickeder we are. Recycling is our salvation. No wonder we're so nutty about it.

Most people believe recycling is not only good for the planet, but saves money, too. Not quite. Actually, recycling costs a fortune. The cost of Ontario's programs is around $100 million a year, and rising fast. Toronto's garbage-recycling program costs $120 a tonne. And now, thanks to the recession, the market for many recyclables has collapsed. In the olden days, when we just dumped the stuff into a hole in the ground, getting rid of our trash cost just a few dollars a tonne. Have you ever wondered why garbage service is being cut back even though your property taxes keep going up? That's why.

You might think that Canada, which occupies the second largest landmass of any nation in the world, could find room to dig another hole. After all, we've got loads of empty space. But space is not the issue. Ritual uncleanliness is the issue. Even though modern landfills are almost as safe as your backyard, no one wants them within a million miles. People think they give babies brain damage. One Toronto city councillor actually called them "immoral." The same goes for incinerators, even though these days they emit less pollution than an '89 Chevy. But don't try telling people that. When one candidate suggested building an incinerator during the last mayoral campaign, another candidate accused him of taking "risks with children's lives."

Meantime, the social engineers are hard at work to make sure we spend even more time picking through our old coffee grounds, sanitary napkins, kitty litter and peach pits. Many municipalities now make people use translucent garbage bags, so that keen-eyed sanitation workers can detect forbidden substances at a glance. The

Taliban had the Ministry for Promotion of Virtue and Prevention of Vice. We have the recycling mullahs.

Like every other citizen, I've had to become an amateur garbologist. If it's Tuesday, I know it must be garbage day. But what kind of garbage? Recyclables or non? Where does the margarine tub go? How about the dental floss and Styrofoam peanuts? Have I forgotten that it's bottle day? Too bad. Now I'll be tripping over my empties for another two weeks.

Every time I think I've finally mastered the rules, the city changes them. And now, every household has been made to buy a garbage bin. All the garbage has to fit into the bin. If you miss a week, you're dinked. You will never catch up! Waste diversion is a good thing, up to a point. But the people who run Toronto think it's the most important thing in the world. As our roads and buildings crumble and our city goes broke, they've decided to spend an extra $600 million devising ways to recycle dryer lint.

But plastic coffee cup lids are an even bigger menace. We Torontonians are crazy about our takeout coffee. And where do we get most of it? Tim Hortons! Tim's cups are made of virtuous recyclable paper, but the lids are made of evil plastic, which means they might as well be WMDs. The lids make the cups impossible to recycle unless you can persuade people to separate the cups and lids when they throw them out. There is an expensive recycling machine that will separate them, but the city says it can't afford one. So now the city wants people to use their own mugs for takeout coffee. It wants Tim's to give them twenty cents off when they do. Right now Tim's only gives them ten cents off.

"The status quo is going to change, and it can't change soon enough for me," roared waste czar Glenn De Baeremaeker, who has persuaded the city to spend \$50,000 on consultants to crack the problem.

The tempest in a Tim's cup has brewed up bitter arguments between the city and the restaurant industry. You might think the dispute is trivial, but it's not. As Councillor De Baeremaeker said at the end of one marathon debate, "I hope we all go home tonight and remember that we all have a responsibility to this planet and to our children."

It never occurred to me that choosing a coffee cup for my double-double is an ethical decision. But now that I'm enlightened, how hard can it be? The answer is that it's a lot harder than you think. In fact, there are numerous websites, engineering reports, and university student subcommittees devoted to measuring the environmental impact of various types of coffee cups. The classic of the genre seems to be a study called "Reusable and Disposable Cups: An Energy-Based Evaluation," by former chemistry professor Martin B. Hocking, who, I am proud to say, comes from our own University of Victoria.

To perform a proper life-cycle analysis of coffee cups, Professor Hocking began by calculating the embodied energy in each type of cup. Not surprisingly, he found that it takes a great deal more energy to manufacture a reusable ceramic cup than it does to manufacture any kind of disposable cup. For every paper coffee cup you use, you'd have to reuse your ceramic mug at least thirty-nine times to break even, energy-wise (assuming that you wash it once in a while). For every polystyrene cup, you'd have to use your mug a whopping 1,006 times to break even.

I trust that clears things up.

The moral of the story, if you are still with me, is that it's a whole lot easier to harass coffee chains, retailers and citizens than it is to do something that actually makes environmental sense. If you want to be a conscientious citizen, just remember George Orwell's novel *1984,* which depicts a world where everything was forbidden unless it was permitted. It all makes me very sad. It makes me feel like lighting up a joint, for old times' sake. I'd never have a cigarette, of course. Too risky. I'm a lot less likely to get busted for a joint.

Chapter Seven

Secrets of Marital Bliss, Revealed

At the advanced age of forty-seven, I walked down the aisle to marry the man who is now my husband. Actually, that's not precisely true. I stumbled across the grass in the backyard of the house we'd owned for years, where our astonished friends and family had gathered to see us finally tie the knot. During the ceremony, I was propped up by the groom, who kept my hand in his iron grip and hoped I wouldn't have a nervous breakdown before I said, "I will." Normally I'm unflappable, but that day I had become unhinged. I am told it took fifteen minutes to persuade me to come out of the house.

Every so often we reminisce about all that. "Every moment of every day since we got married has been utter bliss," he lies. I always agree.

These days, the children of many of our friends are getting married. Although they have never asked for my advice, I feel compelled to give it to them anyway. The first and most important rule for a durable marriage is this: honesty is the worst policy. I'm not saying you should routinely lie, cheat and deceive. I'm just saying that unvarnished honesty is highly overrated.

When I was young, I believed the union of true souls required you to share all your most intimate thoughts and feelings—your doubts, your fears, your detailed sexual history before you met him, your candid views about his friends, his mother, and his habit of leaving his socks on the floor. On no account should you attempt this. The whole truth and nothing but the truth is a recipe for marital disaster. The other person doesn't really want to know these things and will not thank you for telling him. Remember, the very moment when you are most inclined toward candour is the moment you should most resist the urge. For example, anyone who puts your cashmere sweater in the washing machine is obviously a complete moron. I have learned that the moron may not appreciate this insight.

There are also certain times when only one answer will do, even if it's an outright lie. If you ask him, "Honey, do I look fat in this?" and he says yes, then you have clear grounds for divorce. The same holds true if he wants to know whether the sex you had with him last Sunday was the best sex you ever had in your life.

I am aware that these tips for a successful marriage may make us sound like Fred and Wilma Flintstone. I assure you we never expected it would turn out that way. We never intended to become cartoonish stereotypes, trapped in the same old pathetic gender roles that have scarcely evolved since the last ice age. If you can do better, then more power to you. All I can tell you is what works for us. As my husband is the first person to admit, men are simple creatures, really. Generally they respond well to comfort food and shameless flattery about their manliness. In return, a good husband will never, ever criticize your love handles.

Here's another important rule: Although you are just trying to be helpful, the other person thinks you're nagging. This is a hard one to wrap your head around. You'd think a husband would be grateful when his wife reminds him he'd save a lot of money by paying his parking tickets on time. Strangely, he never is. On the other hand, I'm not the least bit grateful whenever he reminds me to watch where I'm going in the parking garage so that I don't bash the side of the car against a cement post again. What does he think I am, an idiot?

Another rule (for women only): What happens in the man-cave stays in the man-cave. Most men need a space to themselves, where they can close the door and do whatever they do in there without you bugging them. Maybe he's smoking a cigar. Maybe he's playing with his little toy soldiers. Maybe he's filling up his cave with old coffee cups and socks and unpaid parking tickets. Your motto is: Don't ask, don't tell and don't complain. Don't throw out his mouldy old brown velour couch. Let him have his space. You can have the rest of the house.

By now I bet you're saying: Enough already. What about his rules?

As it happens, my husband and one of his long-married pals were recently asked for marital advice by a much younger colleague who had become engaged. They told him there were only two rules he needed to know. The first one is: She's always right.

Startled, the younger man asked about the second rule. Here it is: Never forget the first rule.

"But what if she *isn't* right?" he yelped.

"You're not listening," they said.

My husband remembers this rule often enough that I am able to forgive his many sins and trespasses, as he no doubt forgives mine. He has other virtues too. Thanks to his iron grip, I made it through our wedding with my dignity nearly intact. Whenever I feel shaky I know I can count on him to hold on tight. That's a good trait in a husband. If you are lucky enough to find a guy like this, keep him.

Mom and dad could've done it

My husband and I are typical urban homeowners—which is to say, victims of our aging house. A while ago we got up one morning to discover a swampy odour emanating from our bathroom sink. Swampy odours are men's work, so I sent him down to the basement to take a look. Sure enough, our sewer had backed up.

Our dads would have known what to do. We didn't. Instead, we panicked. Four or five thousand dollars later, we had new sewer pipes and a new cement floor in the basement. We also had a notion that we'd been hosed. What should it have cost to fix our plumbing problem? We didn't have a clue. Like most homeowners today, we are at the mercy of anyone with expertise. We're dumb little bunny rabbits in the forest, easy marks for anyone who wants to eat us for lunch.

Don't get me wrong. I married my husband for his congenial disposition and his shapely frontal lobes, not his skills with a hammer. Yet I confess that deep down inside, I expect men to be able to fix things, as our dads did, or at least to know how they ought to be fixed. My romantic fantasies generally do not include billionaires, athletes or handsome movie stars. I dream about Mike Holmes. I dream that one day he will show up at my door in his tool belt and say, "Hey, little missy, I hear you've got a leaky skylight."

"We can't do one quarter of the things our fathers can," one young man laments. Most younger men cannot operate a drill press, a band saw or an angle grinder. They're absolutely stuck when the air conditioner breaks down or the ceiling leaks.

My dad wasn't unusually handy, for his time. But he could build a radio from a Heathkit, sand down, varnish and repaint a wooden boat, rewire a light switch, fix a furnace and hang a door. When my parents added a second storey to our little house, they did all the finishing work and painting themselves. (Only rich people hired painters in those days.) My father-in-law could bag a grouse and field-dress a deer. He was an accomplished woodworker, and made turned bowls and furniture. He once built a canoe. Both dads could make a fire in the rain and had a basic working knowledge of auto mechanics. Clogged toilets were child's play to them.

Our dads were able to function competently in the world they lived in. Their skills were crucial to the daily operation of the family unit. But as we come to rely on cognitive skills to earn our living, our practical skills are dying off. When you can make better money manipulating symbols than you can manipulating tools, it's more efficient to call a plumber than to take apart the sink. Still, an entire encyclopedia of practical knowledge is being lost. As we become more and more affluent, we also become more and more helpless.

The disappearance of practical skills isn't just a guy thing. Cooking has pretty well died off, too, if, by "cooking," you include the menu planning and food prep necessary to produce three squares a day for an entire family, with no microwave ovens and no cheating with takeout. Our moms weren't exactly gourmet cooks. But the meals were always on the table—meat, starch and veg, with the occasional homemade pie and cake, day in and day out. Few people have the time or inclination for this type of work any more, unless they're getting paid for it. That's why the fastest growing category of supermarket food is ready-made meals in a box.

The outsourcing of food prep is the greatest revolution in domestic life since indoor plumbing. You can track the steep decline of interest in cooking by the cookbooks on my shelf (the ones I never get around to using, although I mean to). From the 1980s, there's the classic *60-Minute Gourmet.* From the 1990s, there's *The 30-Minute Dinner.* From 2007, I have an invaluable piece from *The New York Times* called "101 Simple Meals You Can Make in 10 Minutes or Less." I plan to try a few of them, when I have the time.

The trouble with not doing it yourself is that you eventually begin doubting your ability to do it at all. The less I cook, the less competent I feel in the kitchen. And I'd no more try to paint the house myself than I would try to make a dress (although each is theoretically doable). I don't even trust myself to arrange my own furniture. Instead, I call my friend, the interior designer, who is, after all, an expert.

Sometimes my husband and I wonder how we'd survive if the power grid got knocked out for six months and there were suddenly no takeouts, no plumbers and no bank machines to get the money we use to pay for all the things we can't do ourselves. Here's our plan: we'll use our last tank of gas to drive up to the country and throw ourselves on the mercy of our neighbours—the ones with the market garden, the deer rifle and the beat-up pickup truck. Swampy odours never baffle them.

We hope they'll take us in, even though we're useless.

Diary of a demented housekeeper

Somewhere in the bottom of my purse is an electrical adapter plug with slanted prongs. It's been there since last September. I forget what country it's supposed to work in. I could just throw it out. But maybe it will turn out to be useful. I keep meaning to put it in the drawer that has everything, including many objects whose purpose I have forgotten. I keep meaning to sort out this drawer. But every time I start, I get discouraged.

"Conquer the clutter!" promises the cover of my favourite shelter magazine. I'm a sucker for cover lines like this. Inside are pictures of rooms that are neat as a pin, with beautifully designed storage systems and cunning natural-fibre woven baskets, which are what you're supposed to have these days instead of drawers.

Every book sitting on a coffee table in these pictures is perfectly squared off. Every sweater on the sweater shelves has been folded and stacked with military precision. You can tell those sweaters have not a single stain or missing button or moth hole. Every silver platter gleams. Every hardwood floor has a soft and glowing sheen. There are no cobwebs on the crystal chandeliers, no dust bunnies lurking in the corners, no finger marks disfiguring the woodwork. There is a place for everything, and everything is in its place. Clutter and chaos have been conquered and destroyed.

I know this is not a total fantasy because I actually do have friends with houses like this. I imagine they must spend their entire lives keeping them that way. I'm embarrassed to have them over to my place. I'm glad they weren't around the other day when I decided our curtains needed cleaning. As I dragged them off the curtain rods, they threw off clouds of dust. I sneezed and wheezed, and thought back to when they had last been cleaned, and realized the answer was never.

It's not that I don't care about cleanliness and order. I crave it, as the crocus craves the springtime sun. Dirt, disorder and mouldy things blooming in the back of the fridge depress me profoundly. They force me to reflect on the law of entropy, which says that the universe itself is inexorably decaying. It takes enormous effort and willpower just to keep things from falling apart. Keeping a clean and tidy house is a constant battle against entropy, and in my house, entropy is winning.

It's a good thing my grandma's not around. In her day, there was a word for women like me, and the word was *slovenly*. She could sew a missing button back on in half a minute. So could I, if I could find the button. I think it's in the drawer that has everything. It's probably been there for a decade.

Like many women of my generation, I have a certain deeply rooted conflict about housework. It was the foremost symbol of our oppression. Vacuuming and scrubbing toilets were not what liberated women were supposed to do. Unfortunately, there was no one else around to do it, either. So I did as little of all this as I could get away with, and used feminism as an excuse for sloth.

Most men are not much help. Modern men know they ought to share the housework fifty–fifty, and a surprising number are under the illusion that they do. The trouble is, most men's standards are even lower than mine. There's no use arguing over the housework with them. A certain gene in the Y chromosome makes it impossible for them to see anything wrong with throwing their dirty socks in the middle of the floor. They can step over those socks a thousand times without noticing them.

So what's a loving but liberated wife to do? Do you pointedly ignore the socks until he finally picks them up himself? Do you throw them at him in a huff? Do you wait until next Monday, when the cleaning lady will pick them up? Do you pick them up yourself, and nurse a silent grudge? Or do you simply give in and lower your standards? Feminist theory, alas, is silent on this problem.

For these reasons and many more, such as the demands of full-time jobs, housekeeping standards have plummeted since I was a girl. Who polishes the silver any more? Not me. I have no idea how to polish silver, and no interest in learning. Every spring, my mom sneaks over and polishes our heirloom silver coffee set because she can't stand the thought of it sitting there and turning black.

Outsourcing, of course, can cover a multitude of sins. But who is going to climb up the ladder and clean out the ceiling light fixtures with the dead bugs in them? There's only me, and I haven't got around to it yet.

Someday, I fool myself into believing, I'll have the time and focus to keep a proper house. Every spring, when all the newspapers and magazines run their articles on spring cleaning, I conscientiously bone up. "Wash walls, underneath furniture, look for cobwebs, behind pictures, inside closets, inside cupboards, behind the furniture, doorknobs, pipes, rafters, bulkheads, baseboards, door frames and fixtures," instructed one of these pieces. "In the kitchen, take everything out of the cupboards and don't forget to clean door hinges. Remove drawers, taking them out all the way to clean inside and the tracks on which they glide."

Clean the tracks in the kitchen drawers? They must be kidding.

Bravely, I started with the curtains, which I stuffed into several garbage bags and put in the back of the car. Three weeks later I dropped them off at the dry cleaner. Then I began to think about the drawer that has everything (actually, we have several drawers like that), and the closets we can't open because something will fall out. I realized that cleaning the house properly would take a good two months, not including my husband's office, which is a no-go zone. Someday I will get around to it. But not today.

Mired in a techno-nightmare

My husband and I have a brand-new iPod nano. It is a replacement for our iPod mini, which doesn't work any more. After the cat knocked the mini on the floor, it never was the same. Something happened to the shuffle play so that it kept defaulting to early Bob Dylan. Then one day it went completely dead.

We asked around to see where we could get it fixed, but everybody said don't bother. Our less than two-year-old mini (cost: several hundred dollars) is now obsolete.

Our new nano is an incredible device. It's as thin as a cracker and narrower than a credit card. It stores twice as many songs for half the price. It is as magical and mysterious to me as the white man's thundersticks must have been to the original inhabitants of America.

Our broken mini has now joined our sizable collection of technology that is obsolete. This includes all of our CDs (sunk cost: thousands) and our entire sound system, which is connected by wires that run down the floors and through the basement. Now we can get far better sound from a few tiny speakers and a little box. Our clunky big TV, which we bought only yesterday (or so it seems), is now fit only for the Flintstones. They don't even make them any more.

We ought to rip out all this stuff and chuck it in the basement. But where? The basement is crammed with old computer monitors, old TVs, old stereo speakers, old VCRs, old tape players, old tapes, old Walkmans and Discmans and boom boxes and telephones and answering machines and even a Betamax. We paid a fortune for it, and now it's worth nothing. My husband and I are living in a museum of obsolete technology.

Instant obsolescence isn't the worst thing about technology. The worst thing is that it's so fragile. Having a home computer is like having a car that breaks down every other block. Something is always happening to our router, whatever that is. Tempers sometimes fray. There are shouts and tears, and frantic phone calls to the current nerd.

Many nerds have visited our house to pronounce some mumbo jumbo and perform the laying-on of hands. Their average age is twenty-four. They assure us that they have exorcised the demons from our machines. We are like ignorant savages who have summoned the witch doctor and hope his magic is powerful enough to effect a cure. Perhaps it would help to sacrifice a goat.

But I doubt that even that will work. That's because everything we have is obsolete (i.e., more than two years old). We will have to throw out the whole mess and start over. I have my eye on something that's as thin as a cracker, and is so light and small I can tuck it in my purse. I am hoping that, unlike the last one, it won't be completely ruined if I knock my wineglass over.

Even when our stuff is working properly, I'm not too sure how to operate it. Sometimes I accidentally program my cellphone to "silent," then wonder why it never rings. Ever since we got the satellite dish, I haven't figured out how to turn on our TV. I am totally reliant on my husband, and when he goes out of town I'm completely stuck. But why learn? As soon as I get the hang of it, everything will change and I'll just have to start from scratch.

Love is better the second time around

I have a soft spot in my heart for Camilla Parker Bowles. She's a total frump. She has awful fashion sense, and looks terrible in clothes. All dressed up, she looks like a sack of potatoes. Her teeth are horsey and her hair often looks as if it's been styled by a Mixmaster. She is a stranger to cosmetic surgery and Pilates. She looks every year of her age. And she's got a guy who's nuts about her.

Camilla's marriage to Prince Charles was a triumph for post-menopausal frumps everywhere. And Charles's devotion to her proves that youth and beauty are not, after all, what matter most. Most men with wealth and status go in for a younger, prettier, more fertile mate the second time around. Like Donald Trump, they age, but their wives never do. Charles did things backward. He married the younger, pretty one first, and we all know how that turned out. Secretly, he always loved the older, plain one more.

When I was young, it was impossible to believe that the middle-aged were capable of passion. To the young, they only look ridiculous. Now that I am middle-aged myself, I know better. Maybe we can no longer do it swinging from a trapeze. Maybe we can't do it without our arthritis medication. Perhaps the fires of lust don't burn quite so hot. But you'd be surprised at how much heat still smoulders in those dying embers.

Rekindled love is part of a significant romantic trend. The world is full of happy couples who fell in love when they were very young, went their separate ways, embarked on other marriages and relationships that ended badly, then found each other again in mid-life and are living happily ever after.

My friend Susan fell passionately in love with a boy at school when she was sixteen. But there were too many obstacles—geography, religion, parental objections and extreme youth, to name a few. When she grew up, she wound up living for many years with a brilliant and much-older man. He refused to marry her, and eventually she left him. She decided to look up her old love on Classmates.com and found him right away. He was living in the

States, had married, divorced, become successful. They arranged to meet again, and found out their feelings for each other hadn't changed. They were in their mid-forties when they got married and he moved to Canada.

Happy endings like these are the reason Classmates.com has become one of the most popular websites in the world. Some people hire detectives to track down long-lost loves. (I've heard that demand for this service is second only to getting the goods on cheating spouses.) There's something irresistible about rekindling old flames. It's a chance to wind back the clock and take another crack at happiness with somebody you don't have to get to know from scratch—somebody who understands where you came from, and who you were before you built your resumé, your assets and your public face, and before you collected all your baggage. And if you've also collected a few bags and wrinkles, well, so have they.

The idea of stripping bare your soul in mid-life to somebody completely new is as discouraging as the idea of taking off your clothes in front of her or him. The chance of mutual disappointment, to say nothing of humiliation and embarrassment, is painfully high. That's why I always hated dating. Taking a chance on intimacy is considerably less risky when you don't have to start from scratch.

I know another couple who reunited in midlife. They, too, went to high school together, had crushes on each other, then fell out of touch for nearly thirty years. Patrick got married and had a career working in computers, until he got divorced and "out-placed" and decided to become a massage therapist. One day, he saw Tanya in a restaurant in Toronto and recognized her instantly. She recognized him back. She had never married. We went to their wedding a year later.

I like these stories because they are about romantic destiny delayed, and about finding happiness when you least expect it. They are a testament to the permanence of character, and proof that deep mutual attraction frequently survives the ravages of time. I'm not too sentimental about the weddings of the young. (What do they know, anyway?) But the weddings of the old and creaky move me to tears. These people understand exactly how blessed they are. They know that their whole lives no longer stretch out before them.

When I was thirteen, I fell in love with a boy down the street named Rich, and maybe (who knows?) he with me. He carried my books home from school, took me to the movies and gave me my first real kiss. It thrilled me to my toes. I think it was his first real kiss, too. He was a remarkably sweet guy, good-hearted, genuine, responsible and true. Then I moved to Canada and never saw him again. He gave me a picture of himself in a baseball uniform, which I have kept to this day.

I think of Rich from time to time, and I am absolutely sure he grew up to be a good man. I like to think that he'd still like me, too. I'm happily married now. But life is long, and you never know.

Travels with my Happy Buddha

Here's a travel tip for you. Never slip on the ice just before your three-week trip to Asia. After I slipped, I crawled home and watched my throbbing knee swell up like a balloon. My heart sank. "Keep it elevated and don't walk on it," advised my doctor.

It was too late to cancel our trip to Vietnam. "We're screwed," I told my husband. "You can walk around Hanoi, but I'll have to sit in the bar and drink vermouth cassis." Vermouth cassis was what Graham Greene used to drink in Hanoi.

But my husband is undeterred by setbacks. That evening he brought home a cheap portable wheelchair that folded up for travelling. "This will do the trick," he said.

The traffic in Hanoi was terrifying. Imagine 80,000 motorcycles coming straight at you, and you get the picture. But my husband wheeled me through the markets and the temples. My wheelchair seemed to blend in rather well with the motorcycles, bicycles, pedi-cabs, taxis and four-footed beasts that clogged the narrow streets. I felt protected, in a way. Who would dare mow down a middle-aged woman in a wheelchair? In fact, everywhere we went, people broke out into wide smiles at the sight of us. "People are really friendly here," I remarked.

But eventually I realized they weren't smiling at the sight of me. They were smiling at my husband.

My husband is a dead ringer for the Happy Buddha.

The Happy Buddha is one of the most beloved deities in all of Vietnam. He stands for contentment and abundance. He is always depicted with a shaved head and an ample belly. The stomach is considered the seat of the soul, and so the large stomach is an allegory for the Buddha's open-heartedness.

One day at a rural market a man came up, patted my husband's midriff, and said something jocular in Vietnamese. We had no idea what he'd said, but my husband obligingly smiled back. Soon everyone was grinning at us. Smiling women started coming up and showing us their babies. "I can't believe how friendly these people are," I said.

Later, we learned that it's good luck to rub the Happy Buddha's belly. It's supposed to bring you wealth and prosperity. The Happy Buddha is also the special patron of children and the poor. Although my husband is a normal-looking guy, he looks unusual in Vietnam. Nobody in Vietnam is bald (except for monks), but he shaves his head. Almost all Vietnamese people are slender, and he has a modest tummy. The light finally went on when we were touring a shrine that had a Happy Buddha statue. "Happy Buddha, just like you," joked our guide. "Ha, ha," my husband said, deciding to take it as a compliment.

One day we stopped for a beer at a local café, which consisted of a few miniature plastic chairs on the sidewalk. After exchanging a few smiles, the young woman who had served us fetched her baby and plunked him in my husband's lap. The entire family gathered round as the baby cooed happily away. It's not every day your baby is personally blessed by the Happy Buddha.

One day on a beach, a Vietnamese tourist ran up to us and patted my husband's belly enthusiastically. "Happy Buddha! Happy Buddha!" he exclaimed, and ran off to get his camera. Somewhere, his friends are admiring snapshots of him posing at the seaside with my husband.

By now I was beginning to see my husband in a whole new light. So what if he's not as slender as he used to be? Instead of nagging him to get more exercise, I ought to realize how fortunate I am. I am married to a man who brings luck, abundance and contentment. Like the Happy Buddha, he has a relaxed and easy disposition. Obviously his ample middle is not a flaw. It's an asset.

Meantime, my knee was getting better. We didn't need the wheelchair any more, and it seemed pointless to take it home. "Let's give it to a hospital," my husband said, and he arranged for us to drop it off.

We figured we'd just leave it at the door. Instead, we were greeted by a welcoming committee who escorted us and our chair to the cancer ward. There we met a middle-aged man who was very poor.

He didn't have any legs. They had decided to give the wheelchair to him. A small crowd began to gather as the nurses announced the happy news. The man looked ecstatic, as if he could scarcely believe his good fortune. We felt pretty happy too. A doctor made a graceful thank-you speech, and we all shook hands. By now I could imagine what everyone must be thinking. The Happy Buddha had come through again.

Chapter Eight

Schools Making the Grade

In the spring of 2007, a fifteen-year-old student named Jordan Manners was shot dead inside C. W. Jeffreys Collegiate Institute, a Toronto inner-city school with a large number of minority students. The crime shocked the city. How could such a thing have happened? The school board quickly commissioned a task force to investigate the tragedy, and many months later it issued its report. It was a damning indictment of a school system that, it charged, was plagued by violence and racism. No school, it warned, was truly safe. "'Culture of Fear' Plagues Toronto Schools," the headlines blared. As one anguished parent said, "We've become the United States."

Or have we?

It soon emerged that C. W. Jeffreys was not a happy place. The principal had been promoted beyond her competence, and the school was out of control. Kids roamed the halls at will, and anyone could enter the building. A Muslim girl had been sexually assaulted in the washroom, but school officials hadn't notified police.

In fact, gangs and guns are a localized problem, and Toronto isn't East L.A. And yet, after wildly exaggerating the problem, the task force heavily discouraged schools from disciplining kids at all. It opposed issuing suspensions to hard-core delinquents (now known as "complex-needs youth") or transferring them to other schools. It attributed the problems of minority kids in the system to systemic racism and sexism, and demanded more anti-racism training for teachers of every hue and background.

Not once did it mention the increasingly serious problem of unsupervised kids with poor family support who fall in with gangs. In fact, it barely mentioned parents at all. That's too bad, because regardless of racism, sexism or any other -ism, delinquency and failure rates are far higher among kids who don't live in two-parent families. Kids need to connect with an adult, a teacher, a counsellor, a youth worker or a parent who takes an interest. And that's where the system really needs more resources.

In a recent survey on school satisfaction in Ontario, 42 percent of those polled gave the schools a B. One third gave them a C. Only 6 percent gave them an A. Some educators said they were surprised by the mediocre grades. Personally, I'm surprised the schools did that well. Newcomer parents from India and Eastern Europe frequently express dismay that discipline is so poor, disrespect for teachers is so widespread, and standards (especially in math) are so low. As always, the biggest losers are not the children of the upper middle class, but the children of the poor, who have little help at home and no other place to go.

Despite the introduction of literacy testing, the education system generally resists taking responsibility for results. The unions wouldn't stand for it. Teachers rarely get fired for bad teaching, and good teachers aren't rewarded. There are some remarkable educators in the public system but the unions won't hear of merit pay. Meantime, grade inflation is so rampant that any kid who breathes in and out is guaranteed a B.

As for the curriculum, many parents might applaud a British trend. Britain's leading independent schools are about to ditch the national curriculum because, they say, recent government reforms put too much emphasis on "fashionable causes." Instead of lessons devoted to life skills, financial literacy, racial issues, obesity and homophobia—which eat up as much as a quarter of the curriculum—they plan to spend more time on quaint subjects such as spelling, multiplication and key historical dates.

The difference adults can make in kids' lives has been demonstrated in Regent Park, a subsidized housing development in downtown Toronto that's one of the poorest parts of the city. Not long ago, most of the kids who grew up there weren't going much of anywhere. The high-school dropout rate was a catastrophic 56 percent and hardly anybody went to university.

But today the high-school kids of Regent Park are outperforming their middle-class peers thanks to a program called Pathways to Education. The program is designed to give them the kind of support that more affluent kids get—from extra tutoring, to career planning to making sure they have bus tickets. It lines them up with internship programs, helps them apply to college and exposes them to a broader world. And it raises their expectations. But perhaps the most critical support they get is emotional. They are surrounded by adults—many of them unpaid volunteers—who believe in them.

Pathways began as a grassroots public–private partnership. The Boston Consulting Group's David Pecaut called it "one of the most successful programs we have found anywhere in North America." But can it be replicated?

The early signs are excellent. Five other low-income Ontario communities have now launched Pathways programs, with funding help from the province. "They had terrifically high dropout rates and were ready to embrace change," says Carolyn Acker, the programs' founder. In the first year, all dramatically cut the number of "at-risk" kids, as measured by school attendance and credit accumulation. They also achieved high participation rates—as much as 91 percent of eligible students. There are 1,720 students in the programs now, and there'll be 5,000 by the time the current Grade Nines graduate.

The Pathways program starts in Grade Nine. To change the peer culture, it aims to enroll everyone. If all your friends are going to after-school tutoring, chances are you will, too. If your friends start acting success-oriented, you probably will, too. By Grade Eleven or Twelve, Pathways kids are talking about becoming plumbers, carpenters, scientists, even MBAs. David Hughes, the president, says, "What's so exciting is their ambition to show what they're capable of."

How much does it cost? It's not cheap. The current budget is $9.5 million, which works out to just over $4,000 per kid per year. Ontario has kicked in about a third of that, with the rest coming from foundations and the private sector. But the payoffs are spectacular.

Four years ago, when I wrote about the first class that had been nurtured through high school by Pathways, I met a bright young kid from Regent Park named Mohammed Shafique. Without Pathways, he joked, "I'd probably be doing drugs." This spring, Mohammed graduated with a B.Comm from Queen's University. "I got a lot of opportunities with Pathways," he says. "I met a lot of great leaders who boosted my confidence."

I'd like to hear more minority students saying this. In Toronto, four in ten black kids drop out of high school, and the news is even worse for boys. That's why I think Afrocentric education is worth trying. And now, under pressure from parents and activists, the Toronto school board is setting up an Afrocentric school (scheduled for fall 2009) in hopes it will improve black achievement. Most people I know, including some of colour, loathe the idea, because it smacks of the bad old days of segregation. But there is a case for black schools—a case based on providing choice for those who have none. "Africentric" courses within a regular curriculum are just not enough. Trying to empower students by teaching them math lessons based on the patterns of kente cloth isn't going to work. But personal, intense interaction and high expectations might.

A tiny private school called Umoja Learning Circle proved to me that Afrocentric education can work brilliantly in a certain context. The school is in a rather worn suburban bungalow in a Toronto neighbourhood where the news tends to be more bad than good. It has just seventeen students from kindergarten through Grade Six. Its curriculum is an unlikely blend of eco-environmentalism and Afrocentric pride. Its food is strictly vegetarian, and all its students are black and biracial. No need for Black History Month here—black history is woven seamlessly into the curriculum. None of the children's families are well off, and they have to scrimp and save to come up with the tuition.

The black accent by itself is not the reason Umoja works. The school offers small classes, high aspirations, a nurturing environment and a gifted leader named Tafari (who uses only one name). Born in Trinidad and educated in Canada, she started the school when she couldn't get a job teaching in the public system. Tafari aims to build community, self-determination, discipline and respect. "Anywhere I take the children, people ask, 'Who are they?' They're well behaved. They're not fighting," she says. "That comes from discipline." The parents are involved too. They are required to help out at the school, do fundraising and limit the kids' television time. By the time the children leave Umoja, they are equipped not only to excel in public school—they've also got some armour to resist the peer and media culture that tells them it's dumb to be smart and that the most important thing is owning the right Nikes.

No one makes the case for black-focused schools better than Howard Fuller, a former superintendent of public schools in Milwaukee. Dr. Fuller, who's black, is a veteran of Milwaukee's voucher system—a highly controversial program that allows low-income families (mostly black) to choose alternatives to the public schools. More than 17,000 low-income students are now enrolled in private alternative schools, with tuition paid for by the state. Voucher programs are regarded in many quarters as a product of right-wing ideology, but he sees them as an instrument of social justice. "Thousands of lives have been saved because this program exists," he insists. Currently, he's involved with a small, new high school whose goal is to graduate every kid and send them all to college. In the first graduating class, eleven out of twelve students did just that.

Dr. Fuller points out that students who choose black-focused schools already feel estranged from the larger society. The purpose of these schools is to give them a solid sense of themselves, as well as the skills and confidence they need to function in the mainstream. And he is the first person to acknowledge that black-focused schools don't always work. But some do. He figures we won't lose anything by trying. "I'm less worried about the failure of one school than about the failure to educate a large number of young people of colour," he says.

There's a common denominator to the stories of the schools that have worked: Strong leadership. Committed teachers. A commitment to finding out what works, not race politics or ideology. And an organizational culture that's relentlessly targeted on instruction, data and results.

Toronto's public schools provide almost none of this. Perhaps black-focused schools—with a genuine focus on success—will eventually find the way. Let's just learn a lesson from the people who've been down this road. The kids need pragmatism, not kente cloth.

––––––––––

One place in Canada where the schools regularly get A's from parents is Edmonton. In the Edmonton system families are encouraged to go shopping for the school of their choice—a choice that includes a sports school, an arts school, a military academy, a religious school, and Mandarin immersion. All school results are public, schools compete for kids, and the bad schools are shut down. Students there regularly outperform the rest of Canada, and 88 percent of the kids in Grade Three can actually read and write.

"In Edmonton, even billionaires send their kids to public school," says Angus McBeath, who recently retired as superintendent. Today, he advises schools across North America on the Edmonton model.

Mr. McBeath is a passionate defender of public education. He's also a passionate advocate for school reform. "I don't think people realize how big an achievement issue we have in this country," he says. About four in ten adults can't read or write well enough to handle the complexities of modern life. Aboriginals, as a group, lag far behind. And yet, we like to think our school system is pretty good.

The three keys to the Edmonton model are entrepreneurship, accountability and choice. The curriculum is determined by the province, but decision-making is decentralized. School principals control their own budgets and have unusual authority to run their schools and spend the money as they see fit. This is a revolutionary notion. In most places, even the smallest decisions—hire a teacher assistant or repaint the gym?—are tightly controlled from the top.

In Edmonton, parents know exactly how much money every school has to spend and how it spends it. They love the choice. Last year, 57 percent of families sent their kids to schools outside the area where they live. In return, the schools are held accountable for results. Every student in Grades One through Nine is tested every year. If pupils aren't doing well, teachers are not allowed to blame parents.

Edmonton has its share of disadvantaged kids. A quarter of its 80,000 students are lower income, and 7,000 are aboriginal. Mr. McBeath argues that the best social program you can offer kids is literacy. And so the focus on literacy is intense. "We had to give up a lot of traditional things schools were involved in," he says, "because you can't do everything." There's less time now for Christmas concerts and raising money for disaster victims. But the focus is paying off. In some lower-income schools, every child has passed the achievement tests. "These children will now be able to take advantage of Canada as a meritocracy."

The city still has major challenges. Dropout rates remain too high—partly because (until recently) the city had a red-hot economy where a kid with muscles could find a job for $35 an hour.

Mr. McBeath argues that the biggest obstacle to reform is the educational ruling class—the school boards, bureaucrats, principals, and teachers unions. "The ruling class never voluntarily reforms itself," he says. The problem with public education is that it operates like a monopoly, even though it isn't. Affluent families can always opt out. The trick is to keep the affluent opting in—and one way to do that is to recognize that one size can't possibly fit all. In order to increase choice, Edmonton has even encouraged three large Christian schools to join the public system.

Edmonton's success is one of Canada's best-kept secrets—except in places like New York, Houston, Seattle and Oakland, California, which are determined to adopt important elements of its approach. Some Atlantic provinces—where school achievement is the lowest in Canada—are interested, too. Meantime, in Ontario the largest school boards are mired in yet another funding crisis, and a startling number of nine-year-olds still can't read.

But no one is thinking of hiring Angus McBeath. He's too dangerous.

Edmonton's success proves that you can offer school choice within a public school system. And there, the public system works. Too often, however, when I find a school that's doing well, it's succeeding despite the system, not because of it. That was the case with Grandview Elementary School in Vancouver.

Grandview Elementary is an inner-city school. The neighbourhood has a high First Nations population, and half the students are aboriginal. (The school's official name is Grandview/ʔuuqinak'uuh.) Many of the other students are from immigrant families. The kids are poor; many of them live in chaotic and dysfunctional homes. Kids like these often do badly in school. But Grandview is one of the most successful schools in Vancouver, with reading scores approaching those of the most affluent neighbourhoods.

It wasn't always this way. Not long ago, Grandview had the worst reputation in the city. In 2001, only 22 percent of the Grade Four kids could read at grade level. The place was such a disaster that people talked of shutting it down.

What has happened at Grandview should be an inspiration to anyone who cares about Canada's most disadvantaged kids. But it is also a cautionary tale, because the dedicated and entrepreneurial team that saved this school had to break many of the system's strongest unwritten rules to do it. The literacy instruction has a strong phonics foundation. The school courts corporate donors for funding. The teachers create high expectations for all the kids. And the kids deliver.

The school hit rock bottom in 1996, when it was terrorized for months by a man who threatened to kill the staff. The facility seemed unable to recover. Teachers and students deserted it in droves. The remaining kids were out of control. The place was a filthy mess.

A new school principal, Caroline Krause, arrived in 2000. If Grandview was a war zone, she decided she'd better run it like a military camp. "It was a power struggle," she says. Her first task was to establish order. Then she set out to create trust and respect. With those elements in place, the learning could begin.

I've seen other successful schools in struggling neighbourhoods. They share common features. All have strong leadership. The principal and staff act and think as a team. They insist on good behaviour and reinforce the message with positive recognition. The place is clean. The reading instruction is based on phonics and has a lot of repetition. The teachers believe that testing is essential to help them teach more effectively. Also—not coincidentally—the kids love the place.

Grandview's lead primary reading teacher, Wendy Fouks, is a phonics person all the way. She is not neutral on this subject, which is one that tends to bitterly divide the education world. She's been teaching reading since 1975, and for years taught reading to learning-disabled kids. "I've always worked with phonics. I really believe children need to learn how to build strong reading strategies using decoding as a foundation and practising using those skills within meaningful stories." A modest, unassuming woman, Ms. Fouks never thought of herself as an activist. But, she is engaged in an ongoing skirmish with the province's literacy establishment, which argues that any reading system is okay so long as it stimulates a child's imagination. Ms. Fouks strongly disagrees. And she's got results to back her up. In 2003, 90 percent of the school's Grade One students were reading at or above grade level based on the results of the Canadian Test of Basic Skills. In 2004 that number had jumped to 96 percent. Today, 88 percent of the school's Grade Fours and 78 percent of the Grade Sevens test at or above grade level.

Astonishingly, school funding in Vancouver (as well as many other places) no longer is sufficient to cover instructional materials. The workbooks for Read Well, the reading program used for the Grade One students at Grandview, cost $20 a child a year. So Ms. Fouks made a pitch to Starbucks, which came up with a $15,000 (US) grant to pay for the workbooks and other instructional materials. Like phonics, corporate funding is another hot button in the education world. Most people on the Vancouver School Board are strongly against it, but Ms. Fouks figures that, if the school system won't buy the workbooks, then someone else ought to, so God bless Starbucks.

Strong academics aren't the whole story here. During her term as principal, Mrs. Krause was determined to start an after-school program for the older kids that offered both athletics and study sessions until six every night. "The after-school program could get the kids connected to the school, and then we could motivate them academically," she says. She also started an outdoor-education program with hiking, rock climbing, skiing and canoeing—and male teachers to lead it. "Our First Nations kids thrive in the out-of-doors," she says.

When she first arrived, she found that many of the middle-school aboriginal kids had been put into a segregated program that was long on cultural sensitivity, self-esteem and hugs, but very short on literacy. There were no demands on the kids, and they were out of control. Far from feeling self-esteem, they felt like failures. Mrs. Krause quickly shut down the program.

"You can't fool kids," says Ms. Fouks. "They know when they're not succeeding."

The widespread failure of aboriginal kids in the school system is probably Canada's most urgent education problem. But at Grandview they believe that academic success is the answer. Sylvain Desbiens, then Grandview's math teacher, told me that when he started there, he thought he'd be doing mostly remedial teaching. "I never thought we'd be teaching gifted programs." But very soon he was. Today, instead of transferring their kids out of the school as fast as they can, parents are trying to transfer their kids in.

Grandview's emphasis on basic skills and academic achievement, Pathways' program of extra tutoring and adult support, Umoja's involvement of parents and instilling of discipline and self-respect—

these success stories don't need A's from me. They've earned them from the students and their parents. Yet what they are doing seems so simple and straightforward—why can't all our schools do this? Edmonton's adoption of school choice and school accountability shows how some of these virtues can be nurtured within a public system. School board trustees, bureaucrats, principals, and teachers unions—are you listening? We owe it to our kids to help them live up to their potential. And one thing the economic crisis has made clear is that a well-educated workforce is essential to Canada's future prosperity. Without it, we can sit back and watch India and China and Korea eat our lunch.

Chapter Nine

Taming the Wild Frontier

Dear Harry and Sue,

Welcome to the neighbourhood! We're so thrilled you've decided to buy that fifty acres next to us in the country. You'll never look back. You will fall in love with country living in no time. Although we're still relative newcomers ourselves, we've learned a lot in the past few years, and we're glad to pass along the benefit of our experience.

First of all, ignore everything the local farmers say. Farmers are natural pessimists. Ralph told us he took his tractor down to your property a couple of springs ago and it nearly sank in the gumbo. According to him, the runoff comes from three directions. From March through May, your building site is pretty much a swamp. Also, the way you've built your laneway, he says you're going to get snowdrifts six feet high. There could also be a lot of bugs.

But don't worry. You can probably waterproof your basement

so it hardly ever leaks. And by July, your swamp will dry up and turn into cement. Some people up here have too much sand, and some have too much clay. You have clay. Very good if you want to take up pottery.

By the way, forget about that idea you have for planting a charming *allée* of apple trees that blossom in the spring and yield delicious authentic heritage fruit in the fall. Apple trees don't grow in clay. If only we'd known.

Lots of people up here like to give their places poetic names like Lyric Pond, Scarlet Hill or Windswept. You should know that this immediately brands you as a city person. Even if you live here for the next thirty years, the locals will still refer to you as "those people who bought the old Pendleton 50." When they ask you where your place is, and you say you live on Scarlet Hill, they won't have the foggiest idea what you mean. Just tell them you live on the red clay gully where the road keeps washing out.

Here's what you need to know about wells. When you drill your well, you'll strike water. Eventually. Everybody says the water table's sinking because of all the new development in town, but who knows for sure? Some people swear by dowsers to find water but, in our experience, fistfuls of hundred-dollar bills work just as well. If your well driller says you've got good head, don't be alarmed. It's a technical term.

The locals are quite friendly, but there are two worlds up here. People from the city are known as "hill people," even if they live in a valley. They're also called "weekenders," even if they've moved up here years ago and live here all the time. The hottest local issue is the huge seniors' housing development that's being planned in town. The hill people and weekenders are against it, because it will destroy the local small-town charm and lower the water table. The locals are for it, because it will be good for business and the tax base. Lately, there have been snide letters in the paper referring to "the cocktail party circuit in the hills" and "the Bay Street/Osgoode Hall crowd." This means you.

Don't worry about finding someone to blow out (not plow) your laneway next winter. It isn't up to you. The farmers have already divvied up their territory, and the price is non-negotiable. One day, your farmer will come around to introduce himself to you. Hint: It's rude to get right to the point. You've got to have a good chew about the weather first. In case you haven't noticed, it's been very dry, and we sure could use some rain.

With weekenders, the universal topic of discussion is, of course, real estate. Everyone up here is quite ambivalent about the rich people who are moving in. We are afraid they're too rich. Unlike those snooty millionaires swilling Montrachet on their horse farms down in Caledon, we are modest and down-to-earth. We'd never live next to the Eatons, even if we could afford to. We prefer the simple, unpretentious life. And now that we're up here, we don't want anything to change. We trade horror stories about the latest tasteless monster mansion going up across the valley. But, secretly, we love these stories. They mean property values must be rising.

FYI, everybody knows exactly how much you paid for your place. "You won't believe how much they paid," people tell each other. We're scandalized. But, even more, we're thrilled, because that means our place must be worth a pile of money, too. Someday, it might even be worth as much money as we've sunk into it.

It's a great idea to build your own house. That way you can have exactly what you want, and everyone can come over when you're finished and criticize your taste. People who have smaller houses than you do will ask each other why anyone would want that much space anyway. They'll shake their heads and bet it's going to cost a fortune to heat.

We know lots of people who've built their own houses up here. They always tell you there's really nothing to it and it wasn't all that expensive. Here is what we found out: they're lying. But don't worry. One day, your finances will recover. Then you'll start hankering to dig a pond and buy a Kubota tractor. You'll grow tomatoes. They'll be the best tomatoes in the world, and who can put a price on that? Before you know it, you'll be old hands. Somebody will buy the fifty acres down the road, and you'll say, "You won't believe how much they paid."

Well, there's lots more I could tell you, but I guess that's enough for now.

Affectionately,

Your new neighbour

P.S. Don't worry about the cattle operation up the road. You can only smell it when the wind blows the wrong way.

When I wrote these words in *The Globe and Mail* a few years ago—a light, amusing piece for a long weekend in the summer, or so I thought—I never dreamed that they would still be haunting me today, or what amends I would have to make. I soon found out.

Our troubles began when we drove up to the country one early-winter day, after many weeks away. The snow was piled high along the road. It was also piled high across our laneway, which had always been plowed by the obliging farmer up the road. What had happened? We gave him a call, but there was no answer. We rammed our way through the drifts, and called again the next day. It wasn't like Fred to not call back.

After a while I got tired of calling, and tried someone else. Without someone to blow us out, we'd be trapped in our own house when the wind whipped the snow across the laneway. I called one of the Curtis brothers, who said he was too busy. I called the other Curtis brother, who said his son had a hockey tournament. No dice. Finally I called Ray Simpson down the road—a crusty old bugger who was trying to sell his farm to a hill person for the preposterous sum of $500,000, and not a penny less. (He eventually sold it for $950,000 and retired to his dream house in a little hamlet a few miles away.) "Don't you know?" he barked at me. "Everybody's mad about that piece you put in the paper. Nobody's going to blow you out."

As usual, I was the last to know.

It turned out that I had hit a nerve. Just below the surface of the (seemingly) cordial symbiotic relationship between the city people and the locals lurked a stew of simmering resentments, just waiting to erupt. The locals had interpreted my piece as a direct attack on their honesty, their integrity, their business practices and their entire way of life. They had cut out the column, Xeroxed it and passed it from hand to hand. Now it was displayed on refrigerator doors throughout the township—cold, hard proof of what the city people really thought of them.

"You mean you didn't know?" gasped Sue, a city friend of ours who had moved up there full time. "We've all known for months that no one would blow you out." After my piece appeared, the weekly paper, *The Echo,* had been full of letters to the editor denouncing the supercilious attitudes of the cocktail party circuit in the hills toward the hard-working farmers who struggled to make a decent living. I thought my piece had spoofed us more than them. They did not see it that way.

My husband regarded me across the table with dismay. "Well,

at least this time you've only infuriated one township and not an entire province," he remarked.

It was not possible, however, for us to blow ourselves out. We needed a skilful man with a large tractor. If no one would agree to blow us out, we'd be through.

We city people are painfully aware that we would not survive without our neighbours. They are the ones who plow our snow, chop down our trees, bale our hay and dig our holes. We'd be helpless without them, and they know it. I was also mortified to have upset the neighbours. They are nice people, and I wanted them to like us.

In need of advice, I called Ray's daughter, Laura, who lives across the road. Of course she knew all about it. She said it was worth talking to Fred and trying to apologize. Just one problem. Fred wasn't returning my calls. So I sent my husband up the road to knock on Fred's door. My husband told Fred that I was very sorry I had offended people, and wondered if Fred could find the time to speak to me.

The answer was: maybe.

Fred is a man of few words. When he finally agreed to take my call, I babbled on for half an hour, explaining that I had meant to be humorous, and that I had nothing but respect for local people, and I had never meant to suggest that they were anything less than fair and honest, and that my humour had misfired and I was very sorry.

Silence.

At last Fred spoke. It was clear that he had memorized the piece, or maybe he had it right in front of him. He went through every slight and insult. He explained that the snowplowing arrangements were made for the good of all. We chewed it over several times. At last I asked what I could do to put things right.

Pause. "You could put something in *The Echo*," he said.

"Yes," I said. "I would be happy to do that."

I sweated over that letter to the editor. In it, I issued a general apology to the entire township, and to my neighbours in particular. I said that they were fine, hardworking people who command my full respect and that I hoped to live in peace and harmony with them for many years to come. I asked my husband to read it over to make sure I'd hit the right note. He told me it was over the top. So I took a line or two out and sent it to *The Echo*.

The next week, *The Echo* ran my apology in full. We drove up to the country, not knowing what we'd find. Mercifully, our laneway had been cleared.

I called Fred. "Was that letter okay?" I asked.

"I guess so," he replied. And we never spoke of it again.

———

You might think, as the farmers do, that we city people come up here to relax, but you're wrong. We are busy all the time. "What projects are you working on?" we ask each other.

One of my friends is creating a garden the size of a football field that is full of exotic plants you've never heard of. He makes you want to run home to your own pathetic garden and pave it over before he drops by. He's doing all the work himself.

Another friend is a weekend cowboy who spends every spare minute looking out for cattle that might need rounding up. He has a belt buckle that says *Top Hand*. Someone else is growing enough vegetables to feed a village. Another person is building a dry stone wall in traditional Mennonite style, and one is busy stitching award-winning quilts.

My own project is to sit on the porch and thoroughly read the weekend papers, with an occasional run to the liquor store when we are out of Chardonnay. I can't say that because I'd sound like a slacker. So I mention some of my husband's projects. "We spent all weekend clearing trail," I say. Or: "We're making mead."

My husband, unlike me, adores projects. The great thing about living in the country is that he'll never run out of them. He has tried his hand at meadow enhancement, apple orchards, beekeeping, chainsawing, cider-making, and now mead, a honey-based drink the Vikings used to quaff. His mead isn't bad, which is to say, you can drink it without flinching. Most people swear it's the best mead they ever had. Even better, unlike his home-made cider, it doesn't explode in our basement.

But by far our most ambitious project was the pond.

I always did want a pond—a cool, clear oasis into which you could plunge after a hot day sweating over the weekend papers. No artificial chlorinated swimming pools for me. I dreamed of something natural. I dreamed of does and fawns stealing out from the woods at dawn to take a drink. We would have weeping willows and ducks. Friends of ours have such a pond, and ever since the day I saw it, I've been eaten up with pond envy.

Our place was pondless. But so what? We would dig one. How hard could that be? We would pay for it with a modest legacy from my husband's Aunt Eileen. We would call it Lake Eileen.

Now we know that everyone who has a pond also has a pond problem. The two go together, like ham and cheese. And when you try to put a pond where a pond wasn't meant to be, nature will do her best to thwart you.

Country people know this. But city people don't. And so a vast sub-industry of pond providers has sprung up to cater to the fantasies of city people who don't know any better. This sub-industry is run by ex–city-people who give their businesses cutesy names like Wet Dreams. They charge twice as much as country people to dig your hole.

We saw through that racket. We hired a guy named Frank. Frank was as honest as the day is long. Before we knew it, we had a hole that was thirty-five feet deep. Spring came and the runoff filled it up. I could almost feel the silky water on my skin on a fine hot day. Then the water level started dropping. By the start of summer, it was down four feet. Where did it go? We didn't know, but by the end of summer, we had a big ugly dry hole with a bit of scummy mud in it and a few pathetic, parched frogs.

Fred redug the hole. We held our breath to see what would happen the next year. The same thing happened. Fred was a good guy, but ponds just weren't his thing.

We now know the most natural thing for a pond to do is disappear. Our friend Barry's pond, an idyllic spot framed by weeping willows, was suddenly invaded by thuggish water plants. The estimate is $30,000 to drain the pond and rip them out. The friends who inspired so much pond envy had to dredge their pond, at vast expense, when it filled up with mud. Someone else had beavers, who chewed down all his trees when he wasn't looking, and turned his pond into a marsh.

We learned that ponds can be a wellspring of marital tension. Our neighbours dug a little pond, but whenever I ask about it, the wife rolls her eyes and shoots her husband a look that says, *That stupid thing has been a nightmare since the day you thought of it.*

My husband is nothing if not persistent. After we gave up on Frank, he got another guy to come round and take a look. The other guy pointed out that our pond couldn't possibly retain water because the hole was way too deep, the grading was all wrong, and it wasn't lined with nearly enough clay. More heavy equipment arrived to turn our bucolic meadow into a construction site once again. Another year went by. It was just as well that Aunt Eileen, a woman with a prudent attitude toward money, couldn't see us throwing it into a hole in the ground.

Like most of our projects, this one has been hit and miss. Right now, Lake Eileen is almost full. It only leaks a little bit. Instead of deer coming down to drink, we have raccoons, who leave mounds of raccoon poop on the dock. The water's fine, if you don't mind pond scum, and thuggish-looking water plants are advancing fast. Still, we were feeling pretty pleased with ourselves—until we got the ducks.

Before I go on, I should note that city people and country people have very different attitudes to many things—including animals. When I see a deer bounding across a dirt road, I think of Bambi. When country people see that deer, they think of meat. Every year when late fall comes, they put down their tools and take a week off to go hunting. The first thing you learn about living in the country is that if you want somebody to come fix your leaky pond during hunting season, you can forget it.

Country people are not sentimental about animals. For them, animals are either food or income. For city people, animals are lifestyle enhancers. If the local cattle farmers eventually go broke (a not unlikely prospect), the city people will probably pay them to keep a few cows around in order to enhance the rural scenery.

Like many city people, I've dreamed of country life with animals. Wouldn't it be fun to have chickens? Maybe I could get chickens like the ones Martha Stewart has, which lay decorator-blue free-range eggs. We have neighbours who have Percherons, and some who have alpacas, and others who have angora goats. Why not us?

But my husband is unenthusiastic. "The trouble with livestock," he likes to say, "is that you never know when it will turn into deadstock."

My husband thinks animals are too much trouble. Until recently, the only animals we owned were our two cats, and the worms we got as a present, which live in a box in the basement and chew through our potato peels. The worms are zero maintenance, which suits him fine.

Then we got ducks. Two of them. They arrived one morning in the back of a pickup truck. They were a surprise gift from our friend Ralph. I had once admired his ducks, so he decided we should have some, too. They were fluffy, white and cute. Who could resist? Ralph took them down to the pond and hurled them in. When they hit the water, they squawked in alarm and flapped as fast as possible toward shore. It turned out they'd never seen a pond before.

"They'll get the hang of it," Ralph said cheerily as he drove away.

From then on, we became slaves to the ducks. First we had to persuade them to get in the water. Then we had to get them something to eat. The trick was to put the duck food where the raccoons couldn't get it. My husband (who is determined, if not handy) rigged up a feeder from a water jug screwed upside down to a steel bar that hung from a piece of wood that he hammered into the bottom of the pond. We had to wade up to our thighs to put the duck food in it.

Later, Ralph phoned. "Don't forget about the duck island," he said. Ducks, he explained, need a safe place to sleep at night, or else something will eat them. So my husband headed back to town to get some more supplies. He built a raft out of plywood and Styrofoam, and anchored it in the middle of the pond with a rock tied around a rope.

The ducks had learned to swim by then. They did everything

together, two bodies with but a single featherbrain between them. We quickly realized that the raft was too high. They were going to need a ramp.

By now, we were calling Ralph rude names and plotting how to pay him back. (We thought we might surprise him with a pair of skunks.) We went back to town and returned with some screws and brackets, then swam out to the raft with hammers and screwdrivers in our teeth as the ducks quacked at us from shore. We bolted on a piece of plywood for a ramp. Then we chased the ducks back in the water and tried to get them to climb up the ramp. They ignored us.

The next day, we had to go back to the city. "What if they get eaten?" I asked. "Too bad," said my husband, although I could tell he was worried, too.

As soon as I could get out of town again, I made a special trip to check on the ducks. I found them on their island, quacking maniacally and demanding food. They sounded as if they were laughing at me.

Ralph's idea was that we would all fatten up our ducks for Thanksgiving. But the longer we had them, the less appealing this idea was. Were they pets or dinner? It was no contest. I realized I could no more eat the ducks than I could eat the cats. I knew these ducks. Their names were Ralphie and Ralphette.

Ralph suggested we could eat his ducks and he could eat ours. That way it wouldn't be personal. But I knew that wouldn't work, either.

Then, one Saturday, one of them was gone. I don't whether it was Ralphie or Ralphette, since they were identical. We searched the grass and steeled ourselves to find a bloody clump of feathers. But he or she had vanished. I felt terrible. We searched all weekend for the missing duck without success. I imagined the other duck must have been feeling awfully lonely, though there was not the slightest evidence of that.

One cool fall day we caught the duck (not as easy as it sounds) and sent it back to the barnyard for the winter. The farmer returned it in the spring, along with a bill for $64.55 for room and board. To tell the truth, we weren't all that happy to have it back. We'd realized that swimming in the pond was like swimming in a duck toilet, so we'd stopped. The pond now belonged entirely to the duck. Then, one fine summer day, it too mysteriously disappeared.

"The duck is gone," I told my husband. I knew I should feel guilty. But secretly, I felt relieved.

———

Until I moved to the country, I hadn't been on a horse in more than forty years. My adolescent love affair with horses sputtered out when I began to hang around with boys, and I hadn't missed them. Then I got on a horse again and liked it. There was something magical about riding through the woods on a crisp fall day with the iridescent leaves against a dazzling blue sky. I felt like a completely different person.

"You're not a real horsewoman until you've fallen off," my friend Melody likes to say. I always tell her that's okay with me. I've never aspired to be a horsewoman—a word that conjures up daring, athleticism, tight pants, polished riding boots and relentless focus. I like riding horses because it's a great way to be outdoors. Riding helps to clear your mind of city clutter. And sometimes you can ride really fast, just the way you dreamed when you were twelve years old. There's hardly anything you can do for fun that beats that.

It's easy to get attached to horses. They are picturesque and lovable. They're herd animals, like ourselves, but each one has its own temperament and disposition. There's a lot to learn about them, but they're also kind of nice to hang around. Some days they're more satisfying than people.

I started riding a few years ago with a rancher by the name of Crusty. He leads rides for city slickers, which is generally more profitable than raising cattle. When Melody and her husband got horses of their own, I started riding with them, too. Melody's horse was Ace, a tall and handsome fellow with a mind of his own. The first time I got on him I tried to make him go left. He immediately went right, and wouldn't stop until someone came to rescue us. Eventually we began to see more eye to eye, although I always felt he was barely putting up with me.

Melody and Bill loved those horses with a passion. They fenced in their pasture and got a pump to bring up water from the pond. The horse makes the pump work by pushing a lever with his nose. Bill was extremely proud of this ingenious device, but at first the horses didn't get it. So he got on his hands and knees and butted the lever with his head until they did.

One day last fall, Melody and I saddled up and went out riding in the woods, all on our own. She was on Bill's horse and I was riding Ace. I had on my new pair of chaps. As we cantered through the trees, I thought: *Is this really me?* I felt as if I were in some twelve-year-old girl's dream. For a moment, I almost felt like a horsewoman.

Not long after that perfect day, I got a call. It was Melody. There had been a terrible electrical storm out in the country, and Ace and another horse had been struck by lightning. They were dead.

That was when I discovered one hazard of getting mixed up with horses. It hurts when you lose them. As it happens, I was on another horse a few days later. A friend and I had been invited out riding by a hospitable man I barely knew. The day was fine, the pace sedate. The horses were well behaved and superbly trained. We were idling along when an enormous wild turkey exploded from the bush just ahead of us. My horse shied, and I flew off.

Fortunately, I landed on my butt. "I'm fine," I insisted. Then I tried to get up. It felt as if someone had plunged a knife between my ribs. The paramedics were very friendly. They had to bushwhack their way in from the road, carrying one of those long, flat boards that they use for spinal cases. "I'm not a spinal case," I muttered. But the only way to get me out was to package me up. So they strapped me to the board like a mummy, or a nutcase, and hoisted their load on to the back of an ATV. A fleet of fire trucks, ambulances and squad cars arrived to meet us at the road. I wound up in the little local hospital, mortified that I'd ruined everybody's day.

Because we were in the country, the people at the hospital were very friendly. Someone even went across the street to get me a cheese sandwich. It turned out that the doctor had some horses, and so did the nurse. "You've really got to watch out for those turkeys," said the nurse, as she shot me full of super-strong narcotics. "Especially when they're nesting."

Now I had discovered something else about horses. You tend to fall off when you least expect it.

That evening, Melody and Bill and their friends got together and had a wake for Ace. They tracked me down and called me at the hospital. "We want you to feel as if you're here with us," they said. Although I don't remember doing it, they said I burst into tears.

It was a slow recovery. I cracked a rib and bruised my coccyx. I couldn't bend over, so I learned to pick things up with my toes. A few weeks later, I eased my aching body into the car and drove over to Bill and Melody's place. I hobbled up the hill to where they'd buried Ace, under the apple tree in the pasture where the lightning struck. I met Melody's new grandson, born the same week she lost her horse. We talked about life and loss and the unexpected bonds you form with animals. "You're a real horsewoman now," she said as she hugged me gingerly.

"No I'm not," I said. "I'm just a Sunday rider who was thrown by a turkey." Both of us were thinking of the day we might get back on again, even though it hurts.

————

Several years ago, my husband and some friends took up the gentle art of beekeeping. I always thought that this was a peaceable activity—a gentlemanly pastime suitable for retired philosophers and poets. Not so. It's a cutthroat business full of heartbreak, rivalries, ambition and despair, to say nothing of non-stop sex.

The Bee Boyz, as they call themselves (they think the *z* gives them a certain youthful edginess), run a vast honey empire consisting of six hives. For the past few years they have been clawing their way up in the honey competition at the Royal Winter Fair in Toronto. The first year they entered, they finished ninth. That was good enough to get a ribbon, which they took turns wearing. My husband has won a couple of Gemini Awards for his films. But he was even prouder of his one-quarter share of a ninth-place ribbon for his honey.

After that, their ambitions were unquenchable. The next year they finished eighth. The year after that, they soared to fifth. The next year, they vowed, the blue ribbon would be theirs.

Bees are amazing little insects. The males have both an enviable and a tragic fate. Their sole purpose is to copulate with the queen on her one and only mating flight. Sex on the fly! Every guy's ideal!

The downside is that many try but few succeed. As soon as a male gets lucky, he immediately drops dead, his life force spent and his life's purpose fulfilled. The others live on for a while as useless bachelors. On the whole, it's better to be a queen. The queen has sex with as many males as possible, then spends the rest of her life being waited on by everybody else.

But a queen's end can be unpleasant, too. Queens get old, and stop reproducing, and have to be replaced. Beekeepers cannot shy away from regicide. Every so often the Bee Boyz order up a new queen, which arrives in the mail along with a couple of attendants. (This delivery system is known as bee mail.) Then they have to find the old one, who is hiding among 60,000 other bees. Then they squish her.

Beekeeping is ideal for part-time amateurs. Apiculture is not particularly complicated, and the basics haven't really changed since 8000 BC. Unlike cows, or even chickens, bees can pretty much look after themselves. They don't smell, or take up vast amounts of space. If they succumb to some mysterious plague, they are not expensive to replace. The operating costs are low, and the returns are delicious.

One year the Bee Boyz bought a new centrifuge, a low-tech contraption that whirls the honey from the combs. It is set up in a shed, where they like to sit around and plot their strategy. Dressed up in their bee suits, they look like a nuclear decontamination squad. Sometimes they get stung, but they bravely insist they don't mind, even when they swell up like balloons and faint from shock and have to be jabbed with an EpiPen and rushed to the nearest hospital.

Secretly, I think, they're rather proud of getting stung. It allows them to act stoic, to demonstrate that they are able to bear discomfort without a whimper. One day my husband pulled a stinger out of his cheek and explained that the act of stinging eviscerates the bee. He dangled the stinger in front of my nose. There was a tiny blob on the end of it. "See?" he said. "That's its abdomen."

Everyone is worried about the bee blight, but around our area the bees are doing fine. Their new queen caught on. She ventured out on her first (and only) voyage, had sex with ten or twelve lucky suitors who instantly dropped dead, then flew back to the hive to spend the rest of her life laying eggs. The problem was the weather. It rained all summer. Bees don't like working in the rain, and they got mean and cranky. By the end of August there was hardly any honey at all. The crop looked like a bust.

Most years, our problem is not too little honey but too much. Split four ways, our share amounts to a zillion bottles of the stuff. My husband goes around with a few of them in his computer bag, in case he runs into people who might like some. They make great hostess gifts. People always say they love it, but you never know. One time we dropped in on some friends and by accident I noticed that they had a whole cupboard of the stuff. All the other partners had been unloading honey on them too. Even so, we felt hurt.

Our honey is the most delicious stuff on Earth, if I do say so myself. But what really matters is what the judges at the honey competition think. Superb flavour by itself is not enough to win. The Bee Boyz have to score high on the technical side, too. They have to borrow special equipment to measure the moisture content, the viscosity and the colour. They have to triple-filter the honey and let it rest to get the microscopic bubbles out. They must leave exactly the right amount of space between the honey and the lid of the jar.

The honey competition is like figure skating. It is filled with arcane rules that no one understands, and the judging is highly subjective. Also, we suspect that it is full of backroom politics. The

Bee Boyz considered offering a certain emolument to the judges, but eventually decided that bribery is beneath them.

I'm happy just to eat the honey. But men are intrinsically competitive. Making honey is much more fun if you can find a way to win at it. Moreover, the honey competition means that my husband is a serious player. "I don't have hobbies," he once announced, echoing the words of some deep thinker. "I have interests."

Not all his interests work out. The apple orchard, made up of rare heritage varieties planted in a field where an orchard should never be, produced one single splendid piece of fruit before it shrivelled up and died. His experimental project to make ice cider produced two ounces of a vile liquid that reminded me of radiator fluid. One year, he grew the world's smallest fetal pumpkin. Sadly, the Royal Winter Fair has no contest for that.

"Don't worry, Honey," I said. "Your true calling is honey."

This year, as usual, the honey judging took all day. It is done in secret—no outsiders allowed. One of my husband's bee partners phoned every hour to see if the results were in yet. At last they got the verdict: Fourth.

My husband was crushed. "Our honey was perfect," he groused.

"You should be happy," I told him. "It's your best finish yet."

"No one cares who finished fourth," he said. And the Bee Boyz all agreed that once again, they'd been robbed.

———

To celebrate the 150th anniversary of our township, the council erected historical signboards. As we drive around the back roads we stop to read them. All that remains of villages called Banda, Perm and Randwick are these plaques by the roadside. The township's population dwindled steadily in the twentieth century. Then the weekenders began flooding in, snapping up the decaying old farm-houses and paying ridiculous amounts of money for land that's too poor to farm. For some farm families, this is the last generation on the land. There's no money in it, and the kids aren't interested. Besides, city folk will give them lots of money for their view. Some have cashed in and built houses a little farther out, in places the city people haven't discovered yet.

"Is there any place as beautiful as here?" we always ask each other as we watch the sun go down beyond our hillside. Obviously, the answer is no. Last summer, the wildflowers in our meadow had never been so thick, thanks to all the rain we had that spring. Outside our window, the swallows dive-bomb the blue jays and chase them away from the nest where the swallow chicks have hatched. Every spring, we forget the winter we complained about so much.

Oh, sure, like most Canadians we love to complain. Our taxes are too high and our social services are too low. Our winters are too long and our politicians are pathetic. Global warming is melting the Arctic ice. But where else in the world would we rather be? Canada is the lucky country, blessed with more beauty and abundance than any other place on Earth. And, sometimes, we're even smart enough to know it.

Our country! Not bad, eh?

Chapter Ten

How Green Was My Wind Turbine

In the summer of 2007, the floodwaters of the Thames washed away our Cousin Caroline's garden. In Britain, tens of thousands of people were left stranded by epic flooding that cut off entire towns and threatened to drown all of Oxford. What caused the floods? Were they a portent of much worse things to come?

A millennium or two ago, people would have said the floods were caused by angry gods, who were punishing us for our misdeeds. Then science took over, and we blamed the whims of Mother Nature and started building floodwalls. Now we're back to cosmic retribution. We have seen the villain, and it's us.

"Human Activity Altering Global Rainfall Patterns," said the front-page headline in *The Globe and Mail,* which ran beneath a photo of the floods. The story described a new study by scientists from Environment Canada who say they have proof that man-made global warming is already making storms more violent and wet weather even wetter.

The British flooding "can serve as an example of the kind of events we will have in the future," warned Britain's chief forecaster, Peter Stott, who helped write the study. Even the prime minister, Gordon Brown, blamed global warming, perhaps because it provided such a handy scapegoat for the fact that Britain's flood defences, like Louisiana's, were inadequate and poorly coordinated. "Like every advanced industrialized country, we are coming to terms with some of the issues surrounding climate change," he said.

It was obvious that these were no ordinary floods. "The drumbeat of disaster that heralds global warming quickened its tempo this week," wrote Jeremy Leggett, an adviser on renewable energy to the British government, in *The Guardian*. "Behind the gathering clouds the hand of God is busy, writing more bills."

Senior clergymen agreed that the time has come for us to pay up. "We are reaping the consequences of our moral degradation, as well as the environmental damage that we have caused," warned the Bishop of Carlisle (who cited gay-rights legislation as one reason the gods were angry). "We are now reaping what we have sown," pronounced the Bishop of Liverpool. "If we live in a profligate way then there are going to be consequences."

Somehow it didn't seem fair that Cousin Caroline should have to pay up for other people's sins. But that's the way it goes when you've offended the deities. Just ask Noah. No sooner had he built the ark than God flooded the earth and everybody else drowned. Today, it's not unusual to describe the catastrophes allegedly wrought by climate change in the language of divine retribution. Most of us no longer believe in the Four Horsemen of the Apocalypse, or the crude medieval punishments of hell, or the personal wrath of an Old Testament God. We're way too sophisticated for that. Instead, we believe that fire, flood, famine and war (not to mention plagues and pestilence) will be visited upon us by climate change. In either case, the ultimate root of these calamities is the same—human wickedness.

"Like the ghost of Christmas yet to come, [these floods] offer us a glimpse of the possible winter world that we'll inhabit if we don't sort ourselves out," warned George Monbiot, who is Britain's version of David Suzuki, but even more so. (He also admitted, "I can't claim that these floods were caused by climate change.") There's only one way to save ourselves from the ultimate deluge. We must renounce our decadent, wasteful, greedy, wicked, fossil-fuel–consuming ways. "We know what we have to do: Make deep cuts in emissions," preached Mr. Leggett.

Curiously, the floodwaters imperilling Cousin Caroline were by no means biblical in their dimensions. Back in 1953, severe flooding in southeast England drowned three hundred people. There was worse flooding in 1947, too. Even before global warming, Britain could be awfully wet. Who knew?

In my view the biggest problem with the climate debate is its fundamentalist tone. Global warming has become our new secular religion, and not a very pleasant one. The warming-ists insist that climate change is punishment for mankind's wicked, wicked ways. We must repent, give up our lives of wretched excess, and throw our vanities on the bonfire. Doubt, and you are damned. Deny, and you're on the devil's side. This absolutism leaves no room for uncertainty, complexity and nuance.

I've always been wary of any kind of fundamentalism. As a temperamental agnostic, I'm prone to doubts about anything that claims to be the revealed truth. I also believe that people who claim to know precisely how human action can modify the climate—an enormously complex, dynamic system made up of other interacting systems—are as deluded as King Canute. Perhaps we ought to be more humble.

You can believe the earth is warming and still be skeptical that the world as we know it is coming to an end. But to some environmentalists, such doubt is immoral. One letter to the editor argued that compared to Nazis, climate skeptics like me are "potentially much worse. Hitler and his henchmen threatened Western civilization; global warming threatens our entire species and a great many others. If anything, the analogy is understated."

To many people, climate change is proof of mankind's original sin. To be born is to be fallen, because to be born is to pollute. Humankind has messed up the planet so badly that the planet would be better off without us. This idea was the inspiration behind a best-selling book called *The World Without Us,* which imagines what the earth would be like if the human race just disappeared. The author, Alan Weisman, says he wanted to show "how wonderful nature could be if only we didn't mess it up so much." Most of the people he interviewed agreed that human extinction wasn't such a bad idea. "If the planet can recover from the Permian [extinction], it can recover from the human," one ecologist told him. In their view, human beings don't just emit pollutants. We *are* pollutants. Pollution is the chief consequence of human existence. And the best way to reduce our ecological footprint is to not live or breathe at all. Our environmental doom and gloom reflects not so much the state of the planet as a profound cultural pessimism.

The climate "debate" has become so shrill, so political and so polarized that it's impossible for even a reasonably well-informed person to figure out who or what to believe. Politics, ideology and scaremongering are far more powerful in this debate than mere science.

Take the *Toronto Star,* which chastised the Harper government a while ago for foot-dragging on climate policy. The Tories' "shameful strategy," opined the *Star,* "could spell disaster for the world as we know it today." Whew! Who knew we were that important? And the truth is, we're not. Canada accounts for 0.5 percent of the earth's population, and 2 percent of its emissions. Meantime, China is building two new coal-fired generators a week. If Canada disappeared from the face of the earth tomorrow, the effect on our climate would be wholly undetectable.

Most scientists now agree climate change is real. But that's where the consensus ends. Beyond that, nothing about the science is settled. Scientists themselves are deeply split about how alarmed we should be, the nature of the threats we face, how imminent those threats are and what (if anything) we can do about them. On top of that, we face a mountain of political and policy realities— the trade-offs between climate policy and the economy, the truth about how much we depend on fossil fuels for our way of life, and the limits of global action.

A growing number of climate scientists believe that the apocalyptic visions of Al Gore, David Suzuki and other alarmists on the best-seller lists are dangerously overblown. "Some of us are wondering if we have created a monster," said climate scientist Kevin Vranes. Scientists like Vranes represent the broad middle ground—the people whose voices have been all but drowned out by the shouting.

For example, scientists are pretty sure that sea levels will rise, and rising seas will pose a threat to coastal areas. But how much will they rise, and how fast, and where will they rise most? Sorry. We don't know.

"Nobody can really tell you what the probabilities are," says Carl Wunsch, a leading climate and oceans expert at the Massachusetts Institute of Technology. "The probability of another metre of sea-level rise in the next fifty years isn't zero, but it isn't 90 percent, either. And if you pinned me down to tell you what it really is, I couldn't do that."

Robert Mendelsohn is an environmental scientist at Yale who specializes in modelling the regional impacts of climate change. "The drought issues are one of the great uncertainties," he says. "We know precipitation will increase, but we don't know exactly where."

The very great uncertainty of long-term climate impacts is a point that often gets lost in the debate. The scenarios range from mild to severe, but it's the extreme ones that get the ink. On top of that, many scientists say the average global surface temperature (which is the most popular way to talk about global warming) doesn't tell us very much at all about what's going to happen in any given region of the globe. "It's almost useless for what people care about, which is their growing season and how they live," says Roger Pielke Sr., professor of climatology at Colorado State University and the state's official climatologist.

Dr. Pielke is steeped in decades of climate research. He points out that carbon-dioxide emissions are just one of many man-made impacts on the climate. Land-use changes are another. "There are a lot of things that humans are doing to the climate beyond CO_2, and we don't understand them," he says.

We also don't know enough to say with any degree of certainty whether taking action X will produce result Y. "Say you spend a trillion dollars to limit CO_2 emissions. Will you be able to limit the sea-level rise, or droughts?" Professor Wunsch says. "People are asking questions of the science that science can't answer."

Science can, and must, inform policy decisions. But science by itself can't tell us what to do. Figuring out smart policies to adopt is hard, and implementing them is even harder.

———————

Here in Ontario, we're counting on the wind to save us. On Toronto's waterfront stands a mighty wind turbine, its blades rotating lazily in the breeze (at least sometimes). It's a monument to good intentions and civic virtue. The mayor loves it. The premier loves it. All governments love wind power, because it makes them look so green. David Suzuki, the patron saint of environmentalism, compares wind turbines to medieval cathedrals—the highest expressions of human achievement. Wind is clean, sustainable, renewable, free. Who could possibly object?

"It's transformational," said John Kourtoff, CEO of Trillium Power Wind Corp., the day the premier introduced his new Green Energy Act. He promised that this visionary scheme will create fifty thousand green jobs, more clean electricity and a healthier planet for our children. It will also serve as a massive transfer of wealth to wind companies such as Trillium Power. The wind companies will get a guaranteed payment that will probably be at least twice what consumers are paying for their electricity now. The solar outfits will get an even bigger subsidy—maybe ten times more.

Not surprisingly, wind companies from all over are lining up for a piece of the free money. Little citizens' groups have sprung up across the province to try to stop them from erecting thirty-five-storey wind turbines in their backyards. I have wind turbines coming to my backyard, too. I wouldn't mind—if only they made sense. If only they could really help us break our addiction to coal and oil, cut our emissions, and so on. But they can't.

One problem with wind power is, it's not reliable. No wind, no power. No one has figured out how to store the energy from wind. That means you always need a backup source of conventional energy (natural gas, for example) to keep the lights from going out. Wind power also eats up vast amounts of land (to say nothing of steel, cement and new transmission lines). That wind turbine on the waterfront barely generates enough power to run your toaster.

Technologies succeed when they start to achieve economies of scale. That hasn't happened with renewables. We'll need major scientific breakthroughs before wind, solar and biomass will become as cheap and easy to use as oil and coal. "Everything you can think of that is a renewable—or somewhat more renewable—energy option has roadblocks to it, and needs a science solution," says George Crabtree, an energy adviser to the Obama government.

Right now, the best way to cut our dependence on fossil fuels is to focus on conservation. The trouble is, that's boring. A picture of a smart meter simply does not say "visionary."

"Ontario's Green Energy Act could propel the province past California as the most innovative North American leader in the renewable energy field," gushes one renowned environmental activist. Let's hope not. California invested heavily in renewables, until it ran out of energy and had to load up on natural gas in a hurry. Today, the state is disastrously broke, its power rates are astronomically high and manufacturers are leaving in droves.

The biggest advertisements for wind power are Germany and Denmark. Germany has more wind turbines than any other country in the world. But wind can't replace conventional power there either, so Germany is also building dozens of new coal-fired power plants. Denmark, with the largest offshore wind farm in the world, brags that 20 percent of the electricity it generates comes from wind. But more than half its wind power is exported, because that's the only way the system can work.

Expensive wind power makes a lot less sense when the price of oil falls. And the global slump will do more to cut greenhouse gas emissions than all the wind turbines and solar panels David Suzuki can dream of. Twenty years from now, those wind turbines popping up all across the landscape will probably be obsolete.

———————

I'm a skeptic when it comes to the various quick-fix schemes for climate change. But even I would like to be more green. That's one reason we got rid of our SUV. It used a lot of gas and became embarrassing to drive. Anyone who drives an SUV might as well have a bumper sticker that says, TO HELL WITH THE PLANET.

But people who are really concerned about the planet don't necessarily have to ditch the SUV. They can buy carbon credits instead. For only $79.95 (US), you can get a decal from an outfit called TerraPass that says you've offset your SUV's carbon emissions for an entire year—all 13,765 pounds worth. Don't laugh. Al Gore buys carbon offsets by the Hummer-ful. So does David Suzuki. Australian environmentalist Tim Flannery does, too, although he recently confessed to me that he has no idea where his money goes, or if carbon offsets work.

The idea behind carbon offsets is very simple. If you can't or won't cut CO_2 emissions on your own, you can buy credits (usually through a middleman such as TerraPass) from somebody who supposedly will or has. This idea is so hot that the consumer market for carbon credits has reached around $100 million a year. That's peanuts compared to the industrial market, which is projected to be worth more than $70 billion by the year 2010.

How does all this work in practice? Well, there are a few bugs to iron out. When the band Coldplay decided to offset the carbon costs of cutting its latest album, it planted a mango farm near an impoverished Indian village. The ten thousand mango trees would soak up Coldplay's CO_2 and the villagers would sell the mangoes and make money. It all went well until there was a drought and the trees died.

Some other bugs: many of these projects aren't monitored. Standards are a free-for-all. And monitoring costs are high. When the G8 nations decided to offset emissions from their meeting in 2005, they invested in a project to supply energy-saving light bulbs and fuel-efficient stoves to the residents of Cape Town, South Africa. The project cost so much to audit that the local town council wound up $35,000 in debt.

But the biggest problem is that it's usually impossible to tell if offsets really do reduce emissions. What emissions will occur if I forget to send my $79.95 to TerraPass? No one knows. The truth is, carbon credits are the modern way of buying holy absolution for your sins. As Daniel Becker, the director of the Sierra Club's global-warming program, says, "People view offsets as papal indulgences that let them make environmentally bad decisions."

But it's worse than that. According to the *Financial Times*, carbon-credit projects are a multibillion-dollar racket, where many companies profit from doing very little, or gain credits on the basis of efficiency gains they've already made. "Companies and individuals rushing to go green have been spending millions on projects that yield few, if any, environmental benefits," the *FT* said.

As Adam Ma'anit, co-founder of the Amsterdam-based Carbon

Trade Watch, puts it, "The fundamental structural problem is this market is designed to produce cheap credits for corporations trying to avoid regulations." Or, he could have added, for guilty consumers trying to avoid damnation. And who can blame them? Buying offsets on the Internet for $79.95 is a whole lot easier than driving less. Besides, it makes you feel so good!

At the very centre of the global-warming debate is one big misunderstanding—people don't mention this, especially politicians and environmentalists, because it sounds defeatist—and that is the idea that we can actually cut greenhouse gases enough to make a difference. To explain how hard this would be, I called on Roger Pielke Jr., the son of Roger Pielke Sr. and also a leading climate-policy expert.

"'Stop global warming' is a non sequitur," he says. "Any emissions reductions won't have a perceptible impact on climate in our lifetimes. It's quite misleading, what Al Gore suggests, that if we drive a hybrid or change our light bulbs, we can reduce the risk from hurricanes."

The climate debate focuses almost entirely on what's called mitigation (how we can slow down global warming). But climate scientists and policy experts say that in the short term—our lifetimes, and our children's—our most important insurance policy is adaptation. We can build storm-surge defences, stop building in coastal areas and make sure we protect our fresh-water supplies from salination. We can develop crops that will do well in hotter climates. We can do what people have been doing for millennia in response to climate—adapt to it.

Adaptation is not a word you hear much. Activists (and much of the public) think it sounds lazy and defeatist. But the experts talk about adaptation all the time.

Nor is climate change bad all the time. Moderate warming would even have some benefits. Large parts of Canada would become far more pleasant, with longer growing seasons, more arable land and warmer winters. Our energy consumption would go down. The magnitude of the good things could be very large for Canada.

People on the middle ground agree that curbing CO_2 emissions is a good idea. Call it an insurance policy for the long term. But they don't agree on how to do it. Carbon markets? New technology to clean up fossil fuels? "We need to break out the challenges of energy policy and adaptation into many tens of thousands of parts," Roger Pielke Jr. says.

There's another real-world problem. A lot of people believe in cutting greenhouse gases—so long as they don't have to pay. When folks find out that cutting emissions is neither convenient nor cost-free, they tend to change their minds—especially when the economy is collapsing. Britain has faced widespread revolts over green taxes. So has the premier of British Columbia.

Then there's the rest of the world. As we demand more wind, solar, geothermal and biofuel energy, the other five-odd billion people are demanding more oil, coal and natural gas. As we debate the merits of carbon taxes versus cap-and-trade, global energy demand is projected to increase another 60 percent by 2030. China has overtaken the United States as the world's biggest CO_2 emitter. It now accounts for two-thirds of the yearly increase in global emissions. China and India will build a new coal generator roughly once a week for the next twenty-five years. As we ditch our gas-guzzling SUVs, the Chinese, until recently, were buying twenty thousand new cars every day and will likely do so again when the economy recovers. Hundreds of millions of people around the world are joining the middle class, eating more meat, and buying air conditioners and fridges. Meanwhile, two billion people still lack access to electricity. If we try to tell them they can't have it, they'll just laugh at us.

Can we reduce our carbon footprint enough to compensate for all this furious growth? Sure. All we need to do is repeal air travel, cars, meat eating, and most of the conveniences of the twentieth century. Global warming is really hard to fix. As Vaclav Smil, distinguished environment professor at the University of Manitoba, comments, "The speed of transition from a predominantly fossil-fuelled world . . . is being grossly overestimated. All energy transitions are multigenerational affairs. Their progress cannot substantially be accelerated either by wishful thinking or by government ministers' fiats." Stanford's Christopher Field writes, "It is hard to see how, without a massive increase in investment, the requisite number of relevant technologies will be mature and available when we need them."

In other words, if you think it's hard to control the weather, it's even harder to control the climate. It's all very well to say that we ought to lead by example, and do what we can. It's a good thing to start figuring out how we can wean ourselves off fossil fuels. But if all our efforts to regulate carbon amount to scooping sand from the Sahara with a teaspoon, shouldn't we face facts and say so?

If we really care about the planet, there are plenty of problems we can do something about. Two billion people still live without electricity, and three billion without clean drinking water and sanitation. In this century, malnutrition, disease, dirty water and lack of sanitation will kill hundreds of times more people than global warming will. Cutting CO_2 simply doesn't matter for most of the world's important issues.

Feeling good is not the same as doing good. So why not focus on what works, instead of what we think we ought to do? For example, if we decide the polar bears really are endangered, then one thing we can do right now is abolish hunting. Meanwhile, deep cuts to emissions will only happen when alternatives exist at reasonable prices. It's science and technology—not international treaties, or futile efforts to legislate fundamental changes to our way of life—that hold the greatest promise for tackling climate change.

I think it's time to rescue global warming from the moral realm and put it back in the real world of real science, real choices and real trade-offs. And that's a highly moral thing to do. There are lots of things you can do for the environment. You can help protect green spaces and endangered species (even if they're fish). You can eat less meat. You can write cheques to help build wells and toilets for the billions of people who don't have clean water or sanitation. Access to clean water is probably the biggest women's issue in the Third World, since it's the women and the girls who have to fetch it. If you help to build somebody a toilet, you'll be making a far bigger difference than you will by buying carbon offsets. Trust me—you'll feel good, too.

Chapter Eleven

The Way We Live Now

I loved my SUV—even though it made me a gas-guzzling eco-criminal. People used to write and ask why I wanted to destroy the planet. According to my hate mail, my car habit was responsible for everything from smog deaths, to urban sprawl and obesity.

When we bought our SUV—back at the turn of the millennium—we felt like pioneers. It was a new model, and we were the only ones who had it. We told ourselves we chose it for the cargo space. But it also seemed to project a certain rugged yet unpretentious manliness, as well as (we hoped) a bit of youthful *joie de l'esprit*. Soon we began to see our SUV everywhere. All of them were being driven by middle-aged people who looked just like us.

As the years passed and gas prices soared, SUVs just didn't have the cachet they used to. They became too big, too square, too hard to park, too easy to roll over. They started to remind me of the giant shoulder pads I used to wear in the 1980s. I thought those power suits looked great then. They just look silly now.

When it came right down to it, the main rationale for our SUV was our cats, who go to the country with us on the weekend. Sometimes we'd haul a bag of fertilizer in it but, basically, our SUV was a big cat taxi. Our eco-conscious younger relatives thought it was disgusting. As the vehicle became more and more expensive to fill up, I was inclined to agree. Eventually we decided to get rid of it. By then, its value was only around a summer's worth of gas. "Maybe we should leave it by the curb with the empty wine bottles," I said, "and somebody will take it away."

When it finally died one day on a country road, I wasn't very sorry. The era of the gigantic SUV was dead and gone.

But then we had another identity crisis. After our SUV years— what? Were we upmarket city slickers or conscientious ecophiles? Were we Beemer people, Yaris people or hybrid people?

The trouble is, there's no such thing as a neutral set of wheels. The car you drive sends a detailed message to the world, whether you want it to or not. For years, I drove a Civic, which pretty well screams "single, female professional." If you drive a Vibe, chances are you're a middle-income urban dad in his early forties with a big mortgage and a couple of small kids. An Audi A6? You're an older, well-heeled, child-free urban professional who owns an expensive espresso machine. It's not that you are what you drive. You drive what you are.

My husband has always struggled to escape this branding fate. Like everyone else, he likes to think of himself as a rugged individualist rather than a marketing niche. He doesn't like Beemers, Lexuses or Audis. Too pretentious. I tried to talk him into an Audi (this was shortly before half our money disappeared), but he wasn't biting. "Why pay extra for those rings?" he groused.

"So let's get an Outback," I said.

"We can't get an Outback," he said. "Everyone we know has an Outback."

It's true. Whenever we go to a big event in the country, the Subaru Outbacks are lined up along the road for miles. Although the name is supposed to conjure up images of Crocodile Dundee, it's the vehicle of choice for late-middle-aged weekenders who have pets and fertilizer and practical spouses and don't want to drive anything pretentious.

"Outbacks are for sixty-year-olds," he complained.

"But you *are* a sixty-year-old," I pointed out.

"Shut up," he said.

An Outback, to be blunt, is a station wagon—a reliable, ultra-bourgeois dad car. (Come to think of it, my own dad drove one.) *Dad car, dad car, dad car,* it shouts.

The only interesting thing about this car is that it's also known as a "Lesbaru," a nickname it acquired after Subaru hired Martina Navratilova as a celebrity endorser. "*It's not a choice. It's the way we're built,*" said the sales slogan. Today, the Outback has become a lesbian cliché, just as the Austin Mini has become a gay-man cliché.

"So maybe we could get a Forester," I suggested. "It doesn't look like a station wagon, and we can explain that it's not really an SUV."

As it happens, Foresters are the über-Lesbarus. "If a car can be shorthand for the lesbian community, that car is the Forester," says the review on Gaywheels.com. Another fan raves: "Whether we're a lipstick femme or big burly butch, these are the top cars for lesbians."

We caved in and went to the Subaru dealer to look at Outbacks and Foresters. Disappointingly, there were no lesbians in sight—

just another middle-aged couple not unlike ourselves. "The new Outbacks aren't two-toned any more," the salesman said. "They're trying to shake the old-guy image."

Well, good luck to that, I thought. Especially if *we* buy one.

Meanwhile, there was our dead SUV to dispose of. We couldn't just leave it in the gully, so my husband asked the farmer up the road to hitch it to his tractor and move it to our place. They quickly struck a deal—we swapped the vehicle for a winter's worth of snowplowing.

In my dreams, I was tooling around the countryside at the wheel of a slick black Audi, with heated seats and a rearview camera that removes the humiliation of parallel parking. The satellite radio is playing something by Emmylou Harris. In my husband's dreams, he was driving a snappy red convertible—perhaps a Porsche—to the sounds of early Dylan. No room for pets, groceries or bags of fertilizer. But then we both woke up, and had to make a real-life choice. Outback or Forester? Did it all come down to this? Were we really so predictable, so old and so banal?

"I have an idea," my husband suddenly announced. "I'm going to tell people I'm not really a sixty-year-old guy. I'll tell them I'm a lesbian."

––––––

In the end, we got the Forester. It's not an SUV at all, I explain. It's a very boxy car. The cats like it. We feel more virtuous driving it, even though the letter-writers still call me "the gas-guzzling Margaret Wente."

We can change our cars, but some things are harder to change. Like our driving habits. My husband and I are very different drivers. For example, I'm an early merger. When faced with the need to move over, I dutifully fall into line right away, then simmer with resentment as more aggressive drivers pass me by. My husband thinks I'm a wimp. He scoots ahead and sneaks in late. Not *too* late, he insists—just late enough to achieve maximum efficiency without seeming anti-social.

Our parking habits differ, too. I like to drive around and around to see whether I can score a cheap space on the street. Nothing makes my day like saving five bucks on parking. My husband just aims for the nearest parking lot, a habit I regard as unforgivably profligate for a Scot.

His worst habit is honking at other drivers who annoy him. My worst habit is driving into concrete walls in parking garages. "How could you not see that wall?" he said the last time I did it. "It was right in front of you." Perhaps I was still upset because there weren't any parking spots on the street. More likely, it was because he was there. His very presence in the car turns me into a bumbling idiot. If I've got to parallel park, I have to make him promise to close his eyes.

I took all this up with Tom Vanderbilt, the author of *Traffic,* a terrific book that investigates why we drive the way we do, and why many of our beliefs about driving are just wrong. The first topic we discussed was merging. "No one has researched merging habits and gender," he said, "but I suspect more women are early mergers." That makes sense. We want other people to think well of us, even if they're complete strangers.

Merging difficulties are major problems for traffic flow, and they're probably the single biggest source of stress for drivers. They trigger our anxieties about waiting, and uncork all our feelings about social justice. Everybody knows that sinking feeling you get when you run into the tail end of a bottleneck and realize there's roadwork or an accident up ahead. You're trapped like a rat. How long will you be stuck? Why are other cars getting so far ahead of you? How can you retaliate against that cheater scooting up the shoulder? A few minutes stalled in traffic seem like an eternity. So you pull out your cellphone, call your office, and rear-end the guy ahead of you.

"We've sent space probes to the far reaches of the solar system," says Mr. Vanderbilt, "but we have not found a way to make drivers merge with the most efficiency and safety on the highway." Irritatingly, he tells me my husband has the right idea. Late merging is more efficient. If we all adopted late merging—using both lanes to full capacity until the last minute—we might improve traffic flow by 15 percent.

My obsession with cheap parking is another major traffic problem. A shockingly high number of people driving around are simply looking for parking. Researchers found that in one fifteen-block section they studied, people drove an average of 3,600 miles *every day* searching for a parking spot. When drivers slow down to study a likely spot—what's known as "parking foreplay"—they create bottlenecks that go on for blocks.

I've only ever been in one serious car accident (someone else was at the wheel). I do not deserve such luck. Not long ago, I turned left in front of four lanes of oncoming traffic (the advance green arrow had expired) while yakking on my cellphone. (Ontario's new law against cellphone use while driving was clearly designed for people like me.) I've sailed through stop signs and red lights while my mind was a million miles away. I've almost wiped out babies in strollers at well-marked crosswalks. I've backed up into ditches. I've found myself turning into my driveway with no recollection of how I got home. For every time I've been caught speeding, I haven't been caught several hundred other times.

By now you've probably concluded that I'm a terrible driver. But probably you are, too. When you're driving thirty miles an hour, your brain sees an average of 1,320 things a minute. You should be paying more attention.

"We all think we're better than the average driver," says Mr. Vanderbilt. But because we're hardly ever punished for our bad behaviour, we're able to maintain the illusion that we're quite proficient. The truth is that most of us are simply lucky.

Fortunately for me, my husband slips up sometimes, too. I thought I'd never hear the end of it after I drove into the concrete wall. But a week later, he backed into the neighbour's fence and nearly knocked it down. I haven't heard a word about my driving since.

Mark is the helpful fellow at the car dealer who sold us our Forester. Mark is not a car salesman. He is a Senior Subaru Brand Specialist. That's what they call car salesmen now. When we looked at the new cars we also asked if they had any used ones. They didn't. But they did have some that were pre-owned.

In a world where people who serve takeout coffee are rebranded as baristas, no one has a menial job any more. My nephew worked as a Customer Care Specialist, which means he made $11 an hour for talking to people in Florida who called to gripe about their cable. Job titles have become so refined that you have no idea what jobs they describe.

Because of outsourcing—which means, "we found cheaper people to do this"—these specialists seldom work for the same company from which you bought the cable service. Instead, they work for firms that specialize in Customer Care Solutions. If a business offers Proactive Customer Solutions, you can be pretty sure it does telemarketing.

Now that the word *sell* is a bad word, the customer must be extra wary. I remember the first time I got a "courtesy call" from my bank. How nice, I thought. They're phoning to make sure everything is okay! But no. They were courteously offering me the chance to take advantage of new solutions for all my banking needs at a very reasonable fee.

In case you didn't know, hospitals don't have patients any more. They have clients. Think of that the next time you get impatient in Emerg with your broken ankle. The funny thing about health care is, the worse things get, the loftier the language. Health-care bureaucrats love talking about "seamless care," even though the holes in the system are big enough to drop your granny through. You also may have noticed that everybody's now talking about "wellness." Alberta has rebranded its health ministry as Alberta Health & Wellness, in hopes, perhaps, that people will take up jogging and stop getting sick.

Just as title inflation is often devised as a substitute for money, euphemisms are designed to cover up the unpleasant facts of life. Residents of old-age homes are sometimes known as guests, as if they've dropped in for a vacation. Actually, there are no old-age homes any more; they're called assisted-living residences. And the Alzheimer's ward has been rebranded as the Memory Wing.

Today, we no longer have disturbing emotions such as grief and anger, separation and loss. Now we have healing and closure. I am not sure when these terms began to leak from the world of therapy into real life. But now they are ubiquitous. No sooner does some catastrophe strike than people begin declaring that the healing has begun.

I'm not really sure what "closure" is. It seems to be something that occurs once you've healed. It is a highly optimistic concept, because it suggests that with the appropriate interventions all tragedy can be overcome, all grief surmounted, all the raw and bitter parts of life soothed away. It reflects the particularly North American belief that you can get over it and move on.

Healing and closure can often be facilitated by the government. After a group of students died in an avalanche in Alberta a few years ago, someone opined that only a government inquiry could bring closure to the grieving parents. After the premier of Ontario apologized for abuses inflicted many years ago at a training school for teenage boys, several teary victims declared, "This brings closure for me." In B.C., a cabinet minister vowed to bring closure and healing to those who had been abused at an institution for the mentally disabled.

Professional facilitators help, too. No sooner does a sparrow fall from the sky than a grief counsellor arrives to help you express your feelings about it. Some people are old enough to remember the bad old days without these experts. Take the case of the man who, as a boy, witnessed a terrible drowning accident in which twelve other kids died. Fifty years later, he confessed, the memory still bothers him. "The healing process could have taken place a lot sooner," he said, "but we didn't have grief counsellors or therapists or self-help groups back then."

In the brave new world of bafflegab, however, I hate management-speak the most. No area of public life today is safe from the language of the marketplace. Politics succumbed long ago. We no longer have political parties. We have brands, which have images to be either polished or tarnished, and policy platforms that, like toothpaste, are carefully tested beforehand on focus groups. Citizens are treated as consumers who either do or don't like the flavour of the candidate, also known as product.

You might not expect better from politics. But what about good works? The charitable world also has a terminal case of management-speak. The global CEO of Foster Parents Plan (now known as Plan, for marketing simplicity) likes to talk about the importance of "brand awareness" in the voluntary sector. He's got ideas for better ways to "leverage dollars" and "compete for market share." As someone whose market share has been successfully captured by this group, I was relieved to learn that the little girls I sponsor in far-off lands are not simply passive recipients of aid. They are "development actors."

Every civic institution, arts organization and charity is obliged to use management-speak nowadays. That's because they need to reassure their multiple stakeholders that they operate on a businesslike model. They must demonstrate that they are effective and efficient, as well as accountable and transparent. It's not enough to help kids who live in poor countries, or treat sick people, or teach students. Every homeless shelter and hospital, every museum and university and branch of the civil service must have a vision, a mission and a strategic plan. Their managers are made to go on long retreats with professional facilitators in order to come up with these things, which are then enshrined on plaques, highlighted in the annual report and hung prominently in the main entrance of the institution for everyone to see.

Since everybody's vision and mission statement winds up sounding pretty much the same, this exercise may strike you as a phenomenal waste of time. And there's more. Everyone must also come up with tangible deliverables that have measurable outcomes. They must commit themselves to partner with their donors. They commit themselves to empower their clients, customers and, presumably, development actors. Above all, their institutions must be leaders, preferably world-class ones.

The decline of public language into sludge is the subject of a passionate polemic called *Death Sentences,* by Australian writer Don Watson. Mr. Watson thinks words ought to matter. He argues that the narrow, cliché-ridden vocabulary of managerialism has robbed the public language of elegance and gravity. "We use language to deal with moral and political dilemmas, but not this language," he fumes. "This language is not capable of serious deliberation. It could no more carry a complex argument than it could describe the sound of a nightingale. Listen to it in the political and corporate landscape, and you hear noises that our recent ancestors might have taken for Gaelic or Swahili, and that we ourselves often do not understand."

The language of management-speak has created a dark and impenetrable thicket. And once it gets into a place, it spreads like duckweed. "All kinds of institutions now cannot tell us about their services, including the most piddling change in them, without also telling us that they are contemporary, innovative and forward-looking, and committed to continuous improvement," he points out. Much of this abuse originates with management consultants, who, far from being jailed or sued for it, are richly rewarded. By far the worst offenders are HR practitioners, followed by those people who concoct recruitment ads. Like mission statements, all job ads sound the same. Everybody wants a "leader" who is "strategic," and preferably "visionary."

Anyone who cares about language, about meaning, about clarity, should revolt. Citizens are not customers, and democracy is not a product. If Barbra Streisand had sung "Customers . . . customers who need customers," would anyone have cared? If Martin Luther King had said, "I have a vision statement," would anyone have listened? As some wise man once said, what does it profit you if you gain market share but lose your soul? Or something like that.

Chapter Twelve

Rights Run Amok

Gator Ted's Tap and Grill isn't the first place that comes to mind as the new front line in the battle for human rights. It looks like just another restaurant in an ordinary suburban shopping plaza—a friendly spot for regulars to grab a beer after work or treat the kids to burgers and fries. But to the Ontario Human Rights Commission, Gator Ted's is the setting for a possible landmark case for the rights of the disabled.

The villain in this tale (depending on your point of view) is restaurant owner Ted Kindos, a.k.a. Gator Ted. He inherited the place from his parents and has been running it since 1991. The hero (also depending on your point of view) is Steve Gibson, a frequent patron of Gator Ted's—until the day, back in 2005, when Mr. Kindos told Mr. Gibson he didn't want him smoking weed right outside the restaurant's door.

Was that a reasonable request? Evidently not. Mr. Gibson's marijuana was medicinal. He has a licence to toke up in order to alleviate his chronic pain, which is the result of a workplace injury. He argues he's got the right to self-medicate anywhere it's legal to smoke tobacco. Mr. Kindos denied him that right, and that amounts to discrimination because of his disability.

Mr. Kindos says he's got nothing against medical marijuana. But the pot smoke bothered the other customers, who don't think it fits in with the family atmosphere. Some of them just don't want their kids exposed to someone smoking weed with impunity. Mr. Kindos says that all he did was ask Mr. Gibson to keep away from the door so as not to annoy the customers. You might think that such a little matter could be left to the disputants to work out between themselves. You might also think that Steve Gibson has no right to make a nuisance of himself. The Human Rights Commission did not agree. After Mr. Gibson complained, it ordered Gator Ted to show up for mediation.

When Canada's first human rights commissions were established in the 1960s, they were widely hailed as a mark of progress. Their job was to tackle systemic discrimination in our society. The first person to head Ontario's Human Rights Commission was Daniel Hill. (His son, the singer, shares his name.) Those were the days when people of colour faced widespread discrimination in housing and employment, when Jews were barred from the leading law firms and clubs, when women weren't allowed to hold the same jobs as men, and gay men were ostracized and even jailed. There was a lot of work to do.

Today, almost every province has its own human rights commission and there is a federal one as well. They have the power to name and shame, to impose sanctions, fines and remedies. They still have work to do. But these bodies have become the court of first resort for anyone who's got a grievance. They look like courts—but they don't operate like courts. They are basically set up to advocate for the complainants. And unlike judges, some of the adjudicators are anything but neutral. Their employees are major players in the grievance industry, scouring every corner of the land for new wrongs to right and new victims to empower. And too often, they create new victims—guys like Gator Ted and other small-business owners who suddenly find themselves in the crosshairs of the vigilantes.

These days, human rights commissions are especially interested in discrimination against people with mental or physical disabilities. That's how Gator Ted got into trouble. "This case isn't about the marijuana," said a Human Rights Commission spokesperson. "It's about a person with a disability being treated differently."

So far, the mediation efforts haven't gone too well. By the spring of 2009 the case had dragged on for more than three years, at a cost of untold thousands of taxpayers' dollars. "They keep insisting we've discriminated against his disability," fumes Gator Ted. "He's got some kind of spinal or neck injury. Are my entrances too low? Are the doors too heavy? Are the bar stools too low? Have we interfered when he wants to take his medication? No. There is no evidence whatsoever that I have not accommodated his disability."

The problem, Gator Ted says, was that Mr. Gibson insisted on making a nuisance of himself. "We got numerous complaints of this guy smoking dope outside our front door. He came into the bar and stank of pot. There are truck drivers in here who get random testing, and they complained they could be suspended. I got kids coming in for lunch, and he was at the front door smoking a joint. I got a dad complaining his kid had to walk through marijuana smoke."

It's clear there's no love lost between these two. Mr. Gibson, who says Mr. Kindos tried to ban him from the restaurant, denies he lights up in front of kids. "He's throwing me out because the other patrons don't like the smell of me. I think he's just stepping all over my rights to walk around as a Canadian citizen." He says he'd be happy to settle for $20,000. Not surprisingly, Mr. Gibson has become something of a hero to the medical-marijuana and legalization lobby. He hopes to set another precedent by getting the government to pick up his $525-a-month medical marijuana bill.

"If this dispute was about racism, it would have been over years ago," says Stephen McArthur, who was Mr. Kindos's lawyer before his client ran out of money. "But it's the first case involving the smoking of medical marijuana in public." Luckily, Mr. Kindos found another lawyer who agreed to take his case for free.

The vast majority of Gator Ted's customers are on his side. Some of them have known Mr. Gibson for years, and he's not their favourite guy. "When he got that licence, he was in here showing it to everybody, cocky as anything," said long-time customer Keith Hunter. "He said he had a licence to grow it, too, and he said, 'They'll never know how many plants I have.'" Mr. Hunter says he's got nothing against marijuana, medicinal or otherwise. "I've got bad knees and I use it myself sometimes. But I do it in the privacy of my own home when my grandchildren aren't around, and that's the way it should be."

The customers say Mr. Gibson is entitled to his rights. But they're entitled to theirs, too. "I'm asthmatic and I had to walk through his smoke," said Ron Kay. "He just flaunted it." Others raise public safety issues. "I see him driving around, and I wonder how many joints he's been smoking," said Steve Ford.

In other jurisdictions, people aren't allowed to smoke medical marijuana in public. There is no such provision in Canada's legislation. "They basically assumed people would act with common sense," says Mr. McArthur. He thinks the loophole will eventually be plugged.

After racking up $15,000 in legal bills, Gator Ted nearly threw in the towel. The commission offered him a chance to settle in return for a small sum of money (payable to Mr. Gibson). He would also have had to post a prominent sign saying that his restaurant accommodates people with disabilities. But then he changed his mind and decided to fight on. The next step is a full-blown hearing with lawyers and witnesses for both sides. Complainants get legal advice for free, but not defendants. This means there's no incentive for a complainant to settle, and no penalty if he loses.

Mr. Kindos isn't all that optimistic about his chances before the "kangaroo court" tribunal. But he has certainly won over the crowd at Gator Ted's. They think this case is nuts. "We've got one arm of the government spending millions of dollars getting us to just say no to drugs, and we've got another arm saying this guy can do whatever he wants," says Mr. Hunter. "Who puts these morons in this position, that they can make decisions that affect people's lives like this?"

———————

One day I decided to go to a tribunal hearing, to see for myself how it works. Few cases get as far as a hearing. Most defendants are advised to settle during mediation, so that they can avoid further expense and nuisance. There's also a reputational cost to putting up a fight. Settlements determined by mediation are confidential. But a full-blown hearing is open to the public. Many companies aren't that eager to have their names publicly associated with charges of sexual discrimination, harassment and the like—even if they're exonerated in the end. So most of them agree to the shakedown. You've got to be a brave soul to fight.

Dr. Robert Stubbs is a brave soul. He is a plastic surgeon who has a private clinic in Toronto. His name is ideally suited to his trade, because he is best known for surgically enhancing the genitalia of people who are dissatisfied with their private parts. He treats a lot of men who think their penises are too small. But women seek him out too. The human rights complaint against him involved two women he had turned down for surgery. Both women are transsexuals (who are the latest rights group to hit the scene, as we shall see). They used to be men, but now they identify themselves as, and live as, women. They'd already had sex-change surgery. They wanted Dr. Stubbs to do procedures—a labiaplasty and a breast augmentation— that are performed only on women. A labiaplasty is a procedure to trim back vaginal lips that are too droopy or protruding.

Dr. Stubbs declined, telling them that he doesn't do surgery on transsexuals. And that, they claim, amounted to discrimination under the human rights code: he denied them service because they were transsexuals. As the hearing got underway, I wondered what Daniel Hill, Ontario's first human rights commissioner, would have made of it. I doubt that Mr. Hill had ever heard of labiaplasty.

First up on the witness stand was Michelle Boyce, a statuesque thirty-eight-year-old with a lush cascade of curly black hair and the breaking voice of an adolescent male. She described herself as intersex—someone who'd been born with both ovaries and a penis. Although raised male, she said she'd always thought of herself as a woman (despite the fact that in her twenties, she had married and fathered two children in the customary way). In 2001, she had sex-change surgery in Wisconsin, where a doctor fashioned a neo-vagina from her penis and the inner lining of her urethra. This procedure, she said, promised the best sexual outcome, "and the cosmetics were the best that I could see." But the surgery wasn't perfect. One side of her new labia was bigger than the other, and she had a flap of skin that made sex painful. "I was having some issues I wanted resolved with my genitals."

Then she read an article about Dr. Stubbs and labiaplasty. "It was exactly what I was looking for," she said. "And it quoted a good price." It wasn't until she was in the examining room that she bothered to mention she was a post-operative transsexual. At that point Dr. Stubbs (rudely, she says) ended the consultation and invited her to leave. "I chased him down the hall and grabbed his arm and said 'You can't do that.' But he walked away." Shattered by his dismissiveness, she bawled her eyes out on the front steps, then lodged a rights complaint that very same day. Later she got the labiaplasty in Wisconsin, at much higher cost. She wanted to be compensated for the price difference, as well as for mental distress.

During the lunch break, I had a sandwich with Michelle. Her gestures were feminine, but up close, she looked more like a guy than a girl. She had a man's big hands, big teeth, broad-bridged nose and coarse facial skin. She told me she'd be happy to settle for $30,000 or $40,000. Her friend, Jenn Finnan, was the other complainant in the case. Ms. Finnan had been undergoing hormone treatment prior to sex-change surgery, and had wanted Dr. Stubbs to augment her breasts so they wouldn't be going up and down all the time. Jenn, forty-five, was a tall, cheery, middle-aged, overweight woman with thinning blonde hair. She didn't look or sound like a man at all. I liked them both, even though I thought their sense of outrage and entitlement—fuelled for years by the administrative apparatus of the Human Rights Commission—was absurd.

Dr. Stubbs's defence was straightforward. He had no surgical experience with transsexuals. The chest structure and post-operative genitals of transsexuals are not the same as those of biological women, and thus, the complainants' transsexual status was medically relevant. Finally, like any doctor who performs elective surgery for a fee, he had the right (and duty) to decide who is and isn't eligible for his services.

By now you may be asking why so much effort has been wasted on this case, which ought to be a slam dunk for Dr. Stubbs. The answer is that human rights commissions have become self-perpetuating grievance machines. Ontario's commission seems to have regarded this case as a landmark test of transsexuals' access to medical care. Clearly it was no such thing.

Indeed, after lunch the case began to collapse. After a bit of cross-examination, Michelle conceded that she wasn't, after all, insisting that Dr. Stubbs was obliged to perform the services requested, even if he thought he wasn't qualified. And there went the basis of nearly the entire claim. After that, the adjudicator wisely adjourned the tribunal hearing for further mediation. Several months later, Dr. Stubbs was cleared, but the case had hung over him for more than four years. Luckily for him, his insurer paid the legal bills.

But even though the women lost, the case changed their lives. Over lunch, Michelle told me that the demeaning treatment by Dr. Stubbs "had a profound effect on the rest of my life." It inspired her to become a full-time activist. Today she has a government-funded job investigating the health status of the transsexual population in Ontario. She and Jenn also have a small business that's hired by big companies to conduct diversity awareness training, especially around transgender issues. Business is good. They get a lot of work because human rights commissions routinely order businesses to do such training. They have joined the rights industry, and it has been good to them.

———————

Transsexual rights are bedevilling everyone these days. One of the biggest dilemmas is washrooms. Should they use the men's? The ladies'? Whichever one they want? Should they have their own? Small businesses that serve the public—restaurants, for example— ignore these questions at their peril. But it's not only restaurants that get in trouble. A few years ago, a male-to-female transsexual tried to get a job at a Vancouver women's shelter that dealt with a lot of rape victims. The women's shelter turned her down because they had a policy of female-only counsellors. (If you are a woman who has just been raped, you probably don't want counselling from a man.) To be sure, the job applicant dressed and self-identified as a woman. But her stature, voice and demeanour were distinctly mas- culine. The B.C. Human Rights Commission found in her favour.

Few of us would deny that transsexuals have an ordinary right to housing and employment, like everybody else. The problem arises when the rights asserted by one group conflict with the rights of another. Consider the story of John Fulton, who owns a gym in St. Catharines, Ontario. In 2006 he got a call from a deep-voiced stranger who wanted to sign up for his women-only gym. Two days later, he got a visit; the stranger turned out to be a preopera- tive transsexual. Mr. Fulton, perhaps with his female clients' reac- tions in mind, hesitated. A week later, he received a lawyer's letter demanding an apology and a cash settlement. He refused, and is now fighting a human rights complaint.

"I'm probably screwed here," he said, after a mediation session proved unsuccessful. The tribunal will again be called on to decide whose rights come first: the right of women to a male-genitalia–free locker room, or the right of a self-identified woman to get everybody else to adjust to her?

Or what about the case of a mother who wishes to breast-feed anywhere she wants? In Ontario, several women have insisted on their right to breast-feed not just at, but in, swimming pools. The Human Rights Commission recently upheld one such case, and ordered the pool to post signs assuring people that it was a breast-feeding–friendly facility. Another woman was outraged when the pool owner (it was a private pool) asked her not to breast-feed in the pool because the baby might poop in the water. The mother declared: "It was my human right. She violated my human right to breast-feed and I knew that."

Then there's the case of the B.C. woman who failed to get a job after a manager complained that she had a hacking cough and "reeked of smoke." She also had a record of a lot of sick days. She, too, has complained to the Human Rights Commission, on the grounds that she was discriminated against because of her disability—an addiction to cigarettes. The commission has agreed to consider the case.

Human rights commissions not infrequently attract people who make a career out of complaining. Consider the story of Ali Tahmourpour, an Iranian immigrant who washed out of RCMP training school back in 1999. According to him, he was singled out and harassed because of his ethnicity. In 2008, the Canadian Human Rights Tribunal awarded him upward of half a million dollars and ordered the RCMP to give him another chance. "I believe I have a lot to contribute to the force," declared the thirty-five-year-old.

On the face of it, Mr. Tahmourpour's grievance is the sort of injustice human rights commissions were devised to address.

But take a closer look. Instead of getting on with things, the would-be Mountie has spent most of his adult life in litigation. If there's any moral to this story, it's this: complain often enough and, eventually, you'll win. Mr. Tahmourpour's career as a human rights complainant began in 1995, when his job contract as a student customs inspector with the Canada Customs and Revenue Agency came to an end. Even though he was asked back, he declined, because in his mind the experience hadn't been a happy one. He lodged a complaint with the Canadian Human Rights Commission, claiming he'd been racially harassed and given unfair performance appraisals. That claim was rejected. Still, he persisted. Anyone who loses a human rights complaint can ask the Federal Court to order it reheard, and that's what he did. In 1998, the court turned him down. Then he appealed to the Federal Court of Appeal, and lost again.

In 1999, he was accepted by the RCMP as a cadet trainee. He lasted just twelve weeks. Devastated, he went back to the Human Rights Commission. Once again, it rejected him, ruling that he'd flunked out because of poor performance, not discrimination. Again, he took the case to court, and lost. Again, he appealed and, in 2005, the higher court ordered the Human Rights Tribunal to try the case again. It did. And this time he finally got lucky.

The villain of the Mountie boot camp was a training officer (since retired) named Corporal Dan Boyer. The corporal screamed and yelled at everyone, but, according to the claimant, especially at him. He also flunked Mr. Tahmourpour at firearms inspection. He liked to brag that he was "politically incorrect"—a boast that, in the new adjudicator's view, amounted to an out-and-out confession of racism. She decided that the trainee *had* been singled out and harassed for being Muslim.

But firearms weren't his only problem. A female supervisor—someone the adjudicator found to be a highly credible and unbiased witness—had rated Mr. Tahmourpour's communication skills and judgment as seriously deficient. Three of his mates testified that his skills in many areas were so weak they were afraid to work with him in the field. In other words, it's likely he'd have washed out anyway.

That's not what the adjudicator found. In her view, the harassment was so awful that it explained all his other failings—even though evidence showed some of his superiors had bent over backwards to be fair.

Since flunking boot camp all those years ago, Mr. Tahmourpour hasn't exactly displayed the resilience, resourcefulness or self-reliance you might expect from someone who wants to be a Mountie. He hasn't held a job. He got a real-estate licence, but that didn't work out. He qualified to be a translator, but that didn't work out, either. He claims he was too busy fighting his case to look for work. Mercifully, the adjudicator didn't swallow that one. That's why she awarded him only half a million dollars, which was far less than what he wanted—eight and a half years' back pay from the RCMP, including upgrades for promotions. You can be sure that when he goes back to boot camp, his supervisors will be very, very careful. Will our nation be well-served if he becomes a Mountie? You decide.

———

Human rights commissions were set up to deal with discriminatory behaviour. But in the past few years, they have turned their attention to another field entirely—hateful and discriminatory speech. We already have laws for hate speech. But the rights establishment thinks they don't go far enough. And so they have moved in with a vengeance, pronouncing on a host of cases that deal with words, not deeds. They have also created a whole new category of claimants— people who argue they have a human right not to be offended.

Ezra Levant isn't everybody's cup of tea. He's a chippy, caustic guy who likes to provoke. He used to publish a magazine called the *Western Standard,* which proudly took politically incorrect positions on absolutely everything. The *Western Standard* was the only publication in Canada to print those infamous Mohammed cartoons—the ones that originated in Denmark and ignited pro- tests around the world. Everybody dumped all over him for that. Politicians from all parties expressed their disappointment. Book- stores refused to carry the offending issue, and the United Church said that the only possible motivation for publishing the cartoons was "racial hatred." Not a single leading public figure defended Mr. Levant's right to offend.

Then came the Alberta Human Rights Commission, which agreed to hear a hate complaint against the magazine (circulation 40,000). The complaint was filed by Syed Soharwardy, a Calgary Muslim who heads an outfit called the Islamic Supreme Council of Canada. He called the publication of the cartoons "intellectual terrorism." "I am absolutely for as much freedom as possible for the press," he told me. "However, when it comes to my religion, Islam, which is very dear to me—when someone shows Moham- med with a bomb in his turban, it hurts. I am directly descended from the Prophet Mohammed, peace be upon him. So when a person published these cartoons they depicted me—I am taking this personally—as a terrorist."

To be fair to the Human Rights Commission, it doesn't have much choice but to hear the case. The legislation is so broadly drawn that it covers expression that is "likely" to expose a person to hatred or contempt. No one has to prove actual harm—just the potential for it. Nor does anybody need to show that the defendant intended to whip up hatred.

Can someone discriminate against you just by saying something nasty? Human rights commissions have said yes. In 1999, British Columbia's human rights tribunal upheld a hate-speech complaint against Doug Collins, a cranky old bigot whose columns ran for years in a local newspaper. In 2001, Saskatchewan's tribunal ruled against a man who advertised bumper stickers for sale showing two stick-men holding hands with a diagonal line through it.

Alan Borovoy was among the founding members of human rights commissions in Canada. Until mid-2009 he headed the Canadian Civil Liberties Association. He's appalled at what's been happening. As he reminds us, these commissions were set up to monitor behaviour, not speech. "The expression of opinions should lie outside of the commissions' jurisdiction," he says. "We never imagined that human rights commissions might ultimately be used against freedom of speech."

Mr. Soharwardy—who was once a journalist himself—disagrees. "They are saying this is just freedom of expression. But this freedom of expression should not be like the law of the jungle. This must be stopped." He claims to have received overwhelming support from Muslims across the country. "I travel extensively and give lectures every weekend so I know what people think—they were all hurt!"

Marie Ridelle, the director of the Alberta Human Rights Commission, stresses that just because a complaint is accepted, "doesn't mean we think there is merit to it." She points out the vast majority are resolved before the adjudication stage. Every effort is made to get the warring parties to hash out their differences through conciliation (which in this case would be a miracle). "We will be asking hard questions of both sides," she promised. Meanwhile, Albertans could rest assured that their tax dollars were hard at work.

Lots of people are under the mistaken impression that free speech in this country is protected in the same way it is in the United States. This is not the case. America's First Amendment is so strong that it guarantees the Ku Klux Klan or neo-Nazis the right to march through the streets of Jewish neighbourhoods, as they did near the town I lived in as a kid. The First Amendment does not allow even false statements about racial or ethnic groups to be suppressed or punished just because they may "increase the general level of prejudice."

Canada, by contrast, is a pleasantly authoritarian state. "Canadians do not have a cast-iron stomach for offensive speech," said a lawyer for the B.C. Civil Liberties Association. "We don't subscribe to a marketplace of ideas. Americans as a whole are more tough-minded and more prepared for verbal combat."

I confess there is a vast gulf of incomprehension between people like Mr. Soharwardy and people like myself. Try as I might, I find the monstrous offence he feels almost impossible to grasp. To my eye the offending cartoons—which are widely available on the Internet—are bland and innocuous. But even if they're hideously offensive, so what? Given the temper of the times, you can argue that Ezra Levant exercised terrible editorial judgment. But if reprinting these things is a crime, then we're all in trouble.

It was the Internet that saved Mr. Levant. When the time came for his "interrogation" (his word) by the human rights staff, he stood up and delivered a magnificent *j'accuse.* His jeremiad was captured on videotape, which he quickly posted on YouTube. People didn't like the sight of a journalist being grilled by a government bureaucrat, even a journalist as obnoxious as Mr. Levant. They rallied to his side. A few weeks later Mr. Soharwardy, who had always styled himself as the friendly local imam, withdrew the complaint. For what it's worth, Mr. Levant figures this episode cost the taxpayer around $500,000. He, too, incurred hefty legal bills, and soon afterwards, his little magazine went bankrupt.

But it wasn't until Mark Steyn came along that the issue of free speech hit the headlines. In 2006, *Maclean's* magazine published an excerpt from *America Alone,* his best-selling book arguing that Muslims would soon dominate Europe by outbreeding the Europeans. (It was a dumb argument, but that's not the point.) A group called the Canadian Islamic Congress went berserk, and four Muslim law students at York University jumped on the cause. They claimed that Mark Steyn was a racist hate-monger. They demanded equal time to rebut the piece (which warned that the Muslim population was becoming an increasingly powerful force in Europe). What they wanted, specifically, was several pages of free space for their own unedited rebuttal, plus a $10,000 donation. The editor said he'd rather go bankrupt. Their next stop: the human rights commissions. They would argue that the author and the magazine had incited hatred and contempt of Muslims.

Anyone acquainted with the flamboyant Mr. Steyn—or with the editorial policies of any major media outlet—could guess who to put their money on. Nearly every journalist in Canada, of every political persuasion, was outraged that any human rights commission would even consider the case. But the B.C. tribunal did. "You are the only thing between racist, hateful, contemptuous, Islamophobic and irresponsible journalism, and law-abiding Canadian citizens," declared Faisal Joseph, a lawyer for the Canadian Islamic Congress.

After a week of hearings, the B.C. Human Rights Commission

dismissed the complaint. Even so, the proceedings were denounced as an embarrassing fiasco. "This entire process was an affront to our right to free speech and should send a chill down the spine of every Canadian who wants to express an opinion," wrote Vancouver columnist Ian Mulgrew. "Had the agency any sense, it never would have embarked on this sorry exercise. All it has done is expose the human rights process to hatred and contempt, and B.C. to ridicule." Most of the public strongly agreed.

The Canadian Human Rights Commission, too, ultimately dismissed the case. The Ontario Human Rights Commission, whose chair is former Toronto mayor Barbara Hall, said it didn't have the jurisdiction to hear the complaint. That should have been the end of the matter. Nonetheless, the commission published a statement condemning the article as "xenophobic," "destructive," "Islamophobic" and "promoting prejudice."

In other words, the right to free speech is the one right that is of no interest to human rights tribunals. Or, as human rights investigator Dean Steacy put it: "Freedom of speech is an American concept, so I don't give it any value."

Chapter Thirteen

The Botox Years

A woman's life is marked by various stages of coming to grips with reality. These stages always start with denial, as in: other people may get cellulite, but not me. Or wishful thinking, as in: I could run a marathon if I really wanted to, and maybe someday I will.

Then, one day, you see the backs of your thighs and there it is. You realize that, like every other woman, you are destined to wrinkle and grow old, no matter what you do. It occurs to you that you probably won't run that marathon, either. In fact, you're happy you can still run for the bus. You realize you might as well throw out the jeans you grew out of at the age of thirty-two because you're never going to lose those extra twenty pounds. Your self-improvement days are over. Now you're going to need iron discipline just to hold the line. After fifty, it's all about maintenance.

Getting older is like living in an old house. It's amazing how much time and money you have to spend just to keep it from falling apart. You're constantly surprised by hidden problems that have been years in the making. One day, the plumber discovers tree roots growing through your drainpipes, and the next day you've spent $8,000 to get your yard dug out and the pipes replaced. Or the dentist finds a big hole in your gums and goes, "Uh-oh." And for the first time in your life, you're wondering whether your dental insurance covers implants. Not so long ago, implants were the things you could get to make your boobs look bigger. Now, they're the more refined term for "false teeth."

When my girlfriends and I were in our thirties, we took a high moral tone about aging. We looked down on the sort of woman who was so self-obsessed and needy that she turned to plastic surgery to make herself look better. Now that we're in our fifties, we have a different view. We have agreed that a little bit of it is not so bad, so long as you still look natural and don't become a junkie or anything. We don't want to look twenty-five again. No, no, no! We simply want to look incredibly fabulous for our age, like, say, Barbara Amiel.

For a while now, I've been wondering whether I should do something about the new lines on my face—the ones that carve themselves from nose to lips and lips to chin the moment I stop smiling. These lines are just like cellulite, which I never thought I'd get, until I did. Unlike my cellulite, however, they are more public. So I asked my hairdresser, who's an expert on these things. He told me they have an amazing new procedure that gives you a face tuck by pulling the droopy skin up through your ears. He had it done himself, and I have to say he looks quite good. The trouble is, this procedure costs about as much as a small car.

What to do? I decided to consult my friend Debra, who is an expert on anti-aging creams and potions. She once talked me into buying a tiny bottle of super-moisturizer to daub on the skin under my eyes. It cost $105, and I was so afraid to use it that now, fifteen years later, I still have some. Last week I had dinner with her, and I noticed she was looking rested and refreshed. "That's because I go to Dr. G.," she said. "Restylane. Botox. Much cheaper than a facelift."

Secretly, I've looked down on the Botox crowd. But Debra did look good. The next day, I made an appointment to see Dr. G., who has an office downtown so people can drop in for injections on their lunch hour.

As I cooled my heels in Dr. G.'s tastefully appointed waiting room, I read up on all the treatments you can get. There's Nectifirm, which promises a "48 percent increase in firmness in twenty-eight days," and is good for turkey neck. You can get IPL Photorejuvenation, microdermabrasion, photodynamic therapy, and glycolic peels. There's also something called Thermage, which uses radio frequency energy to shrink-wrap your face. I felt as if I had discovered a whole new universe of unmet needs.

"I want you to renew, refresh and revitalize me," I told Dr. G., who prides himself on being an artiste. He recommended some filler and a little Botox, plus several treatments with a laser-like instrument to even out my blotchy complexion and red nose. The filler was something called Juvéderm. He asked whether I'd like to be filled up right away, and I said, yes, of course. He drew a few lines on my face with a pen, froze my lips and chin, and injected me with many needles.

"This resculpts you from within," he promised, massaging my lower face with his fingers from the inside of my mouth.

After he was done, he gave me a mirror. It was hard to judge the effect, because my frozen lips had swollen to twice their normal size. "You'll look like a duck for an hour or two," he said. He also warned that I might drool.

I forked over $2,071 and booked an appointment in two weeks to rejuvenate my blotchy skin.

The trouble with being over fifty is that your maintenance schedule gets more and more demanding, and you're always falling further and further behind. You've got the manicures and pedicures and facials, the exercise classes and the chiropractor, the colonoscopies and mammograms, the haircuts and the colouring, the dentist, the periodontist, and, now, the Botox. You need an army of support people just to keep you upright and presentable.

It's occurred to me that if I attended to all these duties faithfully, there'd be hardly any time to have a life. But letting go is not an option, either. Like a neglected old house, you'll deteriorate awfully fast, and pretty soon you'll be a dump.

After my mouth started to unfreeze, I phoned my husband to let him know I'd dipped into our maintenance fund. I told him not to be alarmed if I came home looking like a drooling duck. Besides, as Debra had said, it's much cheaper than a facelift.

Fortunately, there are some upsides to getting older. For example, something funny has happened to my hair. It seems to have more body.

"What's up with my hair?" I asked my colourist, who collects $160 every once in a while to smear it with chemicals and wrap it up in tinfoil and bake it under a hot lamp so that it will look completely natural.

"Underneath, it's grey," she said. "Grey hair has more texture."

I was thrilled. All my life, my hair has been limp and scrawny, and now it's full of body. Aging has its compensations after all.

To tell the truth, I'd rather be fifty-seven than thirty-seven. When I was thirty-seven, I was always worrying what other people thought of me. Was I smart enough? Was I too fat? Was I interesting, sexy and promotable? If I gave a dinner party, would anybody want to come?

Now I don't care much any more. I figure other people should be grateful if I offer to cook dinner for them. I'm not all that interesting or nice, but I usually manage to disguise it. And maybe I'm a little plump, but so what?

Then there were the gnawing existential questions. Was my career going in the right direction? Where was Mr. Right? Should I get pregnant? Could I get pregnant? *Was* I pregnant? If so, was that good or bad?

I worried about these matters incessantly for twenty or thirty years. Now they have more or less resolved themselves. This is a relief. These days, I worry about whether I am getting a turkey neck, and where I put the car keys.

My friends are similarly contented. The ones who were smart enough to have their children young are giddily free of the burdens of parenting. Their imperfect, wayward, nerve-racking children have somehow grown into mature adults and begun producing perfect grandchildren. When we get together, we never talk about our jobs or our love lives or our next career move. Instead we talk about how we want to work less and play more (if only we could afford to). One friend is trying to talk us all into buying some ranch land in Patagonia and starting a grown-up commune. After a few bottles of wine, this seems like an excellent idea.

Oh, sure, there are health scares. But most of them are not so bad. A while back, I started seeing spots before my eyes. Then I started seeing sudden flashes of light when I blinked. I was seriously scared that I was going blind, so I went to see my optometrist.

"You're not going blind," she said. "You've got floaters and flashers." She explained that my eye jelly is drying up and little pieces of it are breaking off and floating around in there.

Gross! But perfectly normal, at my age. When I asked around, I found out that lots of my friends have floaters and flashers, too. It's one of those things about getting older they don't tell you in advance.

Thanks to reading too much health news, most of us get needlessly alarmed and fear the worst. Catherine, a friend of mine, told me how she once got violent heart palpitations just before a crucial meeting that she had to chair. She thought it might be a heart attack, so she phoned her doctor and told him it was urgent. "Catherine," he said. "You've drunk too much coffee on an empty stomach. Eat something." After a similar experience, I saw my doctor too. "You definitely have heart disease," he told me, and pulled out a giant plastic artery clogged with white plastic fat. "On the other hand, so does everyone your age."

The most annoying part of aging is forgetting where you left things—keys, cellphones, glasses, credit cards. My husband and I have lost three digital cameras this way. Some days I have to look in the parking lot outside my office window to find out whether I drove the car to work.

The most embarrassing part is forgetting names. That's why I've started greeting anyone who makes eye contact with a fake delighted smile and an enthusiastic, "How great to see you!" Have we met before? I have no idea. But chances are, they don't either.

I know there is a logical explanation for this forgetfulness. I have a hole in my brain, and bits of information are leaking out. Or perhaps my brain is simply drying up, like my eyeballs, and little pieces of it are disintegrating and breaking off. I keep going to the drugstore to see if they have something called Astro-Brain, but no luck yet.

At a certain point in life, one begins to realize that virtue consists not in further self-improvement, which is futile, but in holding the line. That's the point I'm at. And then you begin to ask, why are we so hell-bent on self-improvement anyway? It seems to be a fundamental cultural trait. In fact, self-improvement is the defining virtue of North American society. We live in a meritocracy (or so we hope), where class is fluid and people can lift themselves from humble beginnings through hard work and effort to become anything they want. Self-improvement is the modern road to happiness.

Among the most famous self-improvers was Benjamin Franklin (a man of prodigious gifts), who used to write down lists of all the virtues he wanted to acquire. He also commented on how hard it was. "As I knew, or thought I knew, what was right and wrong, I did not see why I might not always do the one and avoid the other," he wrote in his autobiography. "But I soon found I had undertaken a task of more difficulty than I had imagined."

Ben himself was the father of self-improvement literature. In *Poor Richard's Almanack,* he dispensed such aphorisms as "No gain without pain," now the mantra of aerobics instructors everywhere. In its time the book was a phenomenal best-seller, second only to the Bible. Self-improvement books have been clogging the best-seller lists ever since.

I've noticed that men and women seek to improve themselves in very different ways. Men generally want to improve their wealth and status, and so they buy books like *Winning* and *Think and Grow Rich.* (Dale Carnegie's *How to Win Friends and Influence People* remains a best-seller to this day.) Women want to lose weight, find love, and heal their wounded inner selves. In my basement, I am ashamed to say, are cartons full of books devoted to these three topics, the first one especially.

As someone who has gained and lost the same ten pounds for years, I was thrilled when I recently read one of the very latest findings from the U.S. Centers for Disease Control.

Fat people live longer.

That's right. A little padding is good for you. Contrary to what you have been told for years by regiments of health nannies, people who are a little overweight outlast the ones who vigilantly diet, exercise and keep the excesses of the flesh in rigorous check.

Research has found that people who are slightly overweight have a lower risk of death than people who are of normal weight. Thinner-than-normal people are at higher risk than either of those groups. To be at increased risk of death from obesity, you have to be extremely overweight—a category that includes only 8 percent of Americans. These findings are a body blow to the so-called obesity epidemic, which, as we are incessantly warned, is the modern-day plague.

Now that smokers have been taxed, shamed and regulated nearly out of existence, adiposity has replaced tobacco as Public-Health Enemy Number One. So is there *really* an obesity epidemic? That depends on how you define "overweight." As it's currently defined—a body mass index of twenty-five or more—millions and millions of merely moderately pudgy people are classified as "overweight." You can get an epidemic of just about anything if you set the bar low enough. "What is officially deemed overweight these days is actually the optimal weight," sociology professor Barry Glassner told *The New York Times*.

But don't expect the obesity hysteria to go away. After all, fat is the last socially acceptable prejudice. As Wallis Simpson knew once, and Anna Wintour knows now, thinness is one of those indispensable markers that distinguish the classes from the masses. Like smokers, fat people are regarded as hopelessly lower-class. Even the greatest opera singers are now obliged to lose weight if they want to work. And when was the last time you saw a fat CEO?

The fat police are certain they know what's good for the rest of us. And it's not Timbits. They obsess about food the way the Puritans obsessed about sex. These people include not only the nutritionists and dietitians (a profession, I suspect, that attracts more than its share of people with eating disorders), the obesity research industry and the public-health officials, but also the social activists who believe that McDonald's and its fellow manipulative fast-food chains are engaged in an evil plot to poison us for profit.

It's about time we stopped vilifying the flabby, the pleasure-loving, the weak-willed and the slack. So don't worry, be happy, have another Timbit. I now know that I'll never fit into those old jeans again. So what? I'll be content if I can just keep fitting into the jeans I have now. I'll never be the type of person who can get up at six o'clock to jog or get to a yoga class. Such is the acceptance that comes with age.

When I was thirty-seven, I couldn't understand how people who were sixty could stand to be that old. How, for example, could they possibly have sex? Now, I suspect they can—and do. Now, sixty doesn't seem that old at all. It's young enough to still be really good at what you do, and old enough to feel liberated from the tyranny of your inner critic. One day, you wake up and realize that the mortgage is paid off and nothing much intimidates you any more. The background chatter in your head has fallen silent. Somehow, without noticing, you've grown up into the person you were always meant to be. And to your immense surprise, she's not too bad.

Chapter Fourteen

Gazing into the Sunset

I have seen my future, and yours, too. Just drop by your local supermarket any Thursday morning around nine. That's when my mom and I go grocery shopping. I'm usually the youngest shopper there. Most of the customers are around seventy-five.

Early Thursday morning is popular with the older set, because the store isn't too busy, and you don't have to worry about being knocked over. You can get a real bargain on meat that's near its sell-by date. And the guy who knows where everything is has time to find the canned artichokes for you.

There are people with canes, people with walkers and people riding in motorized carts. We usually see a little white-haired woman in her sixties with her even littler mother, who must be ninety. The elderly women tend to come in pairs, to prop each other up, or perhaps to keep each other from getting lost somewhere in the petfood aisle. Most of them are regulars, and we wave to one another, and smile and say hello.

When Mom had major surgery, half the cashiers knew about it. The first time she was well enough to go shopping again, her favourite cashier welcomed her back by name, and a kindly man riding in a cart fetched her cane after she left it behind near the bananas.

My mom is luckier than some. She has kids living nearby who can take her to the store (she doesn't drive any more) and help her lug her groceries home. A lot of people don't.

Mom's illness taught me about all the little things that can strip you of your independence. Shopping bags you can't lift any more. Stairs you can't go down, and laundry you can't do because the washing machine is in the basement. Garbage you can no longer manage to haul to the end of the driveway by yourself, a kitty-litter box you can't stoop over to clean, a bank machine that's too far away, and shoes that no longer fit because your feet are swollen. Daily life becomes a job of mapping out your strategies just so you can get by.

After Mom got out of the hospital, she hired a home-care worker for a few hours a day. You can get home care paid for by the province, but only if you need help to have a bath. That's the rule in Ontario. Her home-care worker was an agreeable woman named Mira, who did the laundry, changed the bed, ran errands and took the garbage out. Mom met Mira in the grocery store, before she had her surgery, when Mira was helping someone else with the shopping. Like many home-care workers, Mira is an immigrant. She's from Somalia, wears a headscarf, and has four children. For many of her clients, she's all that stands between independence and an institution. She likes working for my mother, she says, because so many of her clients get sicker and sicker and finally die, and

Mom is getting better. Someday, someone like Mira will no doubt be taking care of me.

I used to think old age was something that struck you suddenly. One day you'd wake up and discover you were old. It's the same fantasy you have as a child, that one day you'll turn sixteen or eighteen or twenty-one, and suddenly be all grown up. But it's not like that at all. Aging—the gradual loss of power and control over your own life—creeps up on you. And the arrow isn't always straight. Maybe some miracle of modern medicine will buy you an extra decade or two of independence, as I hope it has for my mom. Or maybe senility will rob you of your capacity for life long before your body wears out. Maybe you'll have a spouse to look after you when you get shaky, or maybe not. Maybe your kids will be attentive, or maybe they'll be far away, or maybe, like me, you don't have any. Who will come to fetch my ailing carcass from the hospital when I'm my mom's age? I have no idea.

I've always thought of grocery shopping as an irritating nuisance. But now, I see that someday it will be something else entirely—a mark of achievement and of rugged self-sufficiency. As long as you can make your way up and down the aisle and remember what you came for, you still have your independence and your dignity. That is no small thing. It's the one big thing.

Every week now, when I go shopping with my mom, I realize that I'm one week closer to the time I join the Thursday Club. Maybe it will take another fifteen years, or maybe twenty, but that time no longer seems so far away. At any rate, I'll have lots of company. I can see us now, racing (slowly) through the aisles with our walkers, our carts and our metal hips to beat one another to the discount, organic, free-range lamb chops, our tottering bodies steadied (if we can afford it) by kind people from developing countries.

We talk a lot about the implications of the coming age-wave. But it's just words. I don't think we have a clue what it will really mean, or how we're going to cope, when we are all ready to join the Thursday Club.

The obituary pages these days are scattered with photographs of men in Second World War uniforms. These pictures remind me of how the war helped define my parents' generation and how far it seems from my own. War is deeply out of favour now. We prefer peacekeeping. The warrior values—discipline, sacrifice, cohesion, strength, authority—seem antique, except perhaps in sports. Modern wars are small, murky, troublesome affairs that operate somewhere on the periphery of our lives. They certainly don't inspire much patriotism, another old-fashioned virtue that has become faintly suspect. In our age, our greatest upwelling of national pride was inspired by a beer commercial.

Both my father and my grandfather went to war. Back then, that was what young men did. For many of them, it was both the worst time and the best time of their lives. My American grandfather, Charlie McNeill, couldn't wait to go to war. In 1914, he crossed the border to sign up with the Canadian Highlanders. He was nineteen. But he was already a man. His father had been killed in a railway accident when he was just eleven, and he had to quit school to become the family breadwinner. Compared to hard labour in the slums of Chicago, a chance to see the world for free looked pretty good.

Grandpa was a long, lean and lighthearted man. After he was shipped back with a bullet wound in his leg, he joined up again, this time with the Americans. He wrote jaunty letters home about the rations, the mud and the body lice. "I don't think you would want any soldiers if you had to take them just as they come after a stay on the line," he wrote his sister. "Yes, I've had the cooties three times. . . .When I get a clean suit of underwear and bath I feel as if I could win the war alone."

That time, he came home with a more serious injury, one that turned him into a more serious man. In the last days of the war, an exploding shell had permanently destroyed his hearing. But he had good luck too. He played poker on the troopship all the way home, and landed back in the United States with $2,000 in his pocket. A few years later he took a lip-reading course and fell in love with his teacher, Carrie. She too was deaf. She became my grandma, and their only child, Barbara, became my mother.

My grandparents got married in 1923. She had a university degree, and her family thought Charlie was beneath her. Even worse, he was a Catholic. They were nasty to him, and she never forgave them for that. My grandmother and her sister didn't speak for years, although I didn't find out why until after they were dead.

My mom, an only child, adored her dad. He taught her "It's a Long Way to Tipperary" and told her war stories—but just the amusing bits about the cooties and the food. During the Depression, he got a job building roads for the WPA (Works Progress Administration). He would take her for long walks and show her the curbs and pavement where he'd inscribed his initials in the cement. Eventually, he got a job writing for a technical magazine, and climbed into the white-collar class at last. From then on, he always wore a coat and tie, and he always looked immaculate.

It's easy to forget how short the time was between the wars. The next one started when my mother was still in grade school. In high school, she met my dad, Bill, who was two years ahead of her. In case any enemy spies had infiltrated their tranquil town near Chicago, the hallways of their school had posters warning the students not to give away war secrets. LOOSE LIPS SINK SHIPS, the posters said. Everybody knew the boys would be going off to war as soon as they graduated.

In 1943, Bill was shipped off to the Pacific. He had been a pampered child. Now he was slogging through the jungle with a bunch of other eighteen-year-olds, contracting malaria and jungle rot. Did my father want to fight? "It wasn't a question people asked then," says my mom. "You just did it."

Dad never said much about the war when we kids were young. When he did, he made it sound like a chapter straight out of *Catch-22*, a book of which he was particularly fond. But in the two or three years before he died his war memories sometimes seemed to obsess him, like an old film reel playing over and over in his head. He would remember how the "Japs" were all around them in the jungle but you could never see them, and he'd recall the time they stumbled on an enemy camp so recently deserted that the abandoned food was still warm. One time, for no good reason, he threw himself into a ditch, and a second later a grenade exploded where he'd just been.

He was an old man before he ever talked about these things. For him, the Occupation was more fun. The Americans thought the defeated Japanese would be dangerous and hostile, but instead everybody bowed. Dad and his buddies managed to get their hands on a defunct brewery and got it operating again, bootlegging the proceeds to thirsty GIs for fun and profit.

There will never be a war like that again. The basics of the thing were pretty clear. The practical and moral grounds for war were beyond dispute. Civilization really was at stake. Everyone had sons, uncles, brothers, cousins in uniform. Everyone had ration coupons.

Everyone collected scrap and knitted socks and wrote letters to the front. People were united in a common cause in a way they never are in peacetime.

Everybody in my parents' generation remembers the legendary battles of the Second World War—D-Day and Iwo Jima, the Battle of Britain and the Battle of the Bulge. But who will remember the battle of Panjwai? No more than a handful of us. Future generations will not demand any state funerals for the last veterans of the Kosovo or Afghan wars. The men and women who fought in those forgotten skirmishes are likely to be forgotten too.

My parents' war shaped the destinies of an entire generation. One young man from the Eastern Townships, named Hector McLeod, spent his entire war in Canada, training farm kids to fly airplanes. He was good with his hands, and if it hadn't been for the war, he would have spent his life as a tool-and-die maker. Instead, when the war ended he went to university for free, and became a dentist. The war vaulted him and millions of other young men from the working to the middle class. As a respected professional, he proudly wore a tie until the day he died. His only son grew up and married me. In a way, you could say the war was the best thing that ever happened to him.

My dad came home from the Pacific physically unscathed, except for recurring bouts of malaria that would plague him from time to time. He hadn't dated my mom much before the war, but they wrote each other when he was overseas. She was away at university when he came home, so he dropped around to see her father. The two vets traded war stories, and hit it off right away. My parents married in 1947 and lived on the GI Bill. They moved in with my grandparents and began to make their contribution to the enormous post-war baby boom, starting with me.

When I was growing up, everybody in America was a patriot. The day Douglas MacArthur came to town, my mom put me in a stroller and the entire family went to the parade. My grandma found us a front-row place. There was a big brass band, and I waved a little flag. Not far from the spot where the great man passed by, there was a piece of pavement that bore my grandfather's initials.

When I got older, I would march with the Girl Scouts in the Memorial Day parade, and my grandfather would march with the vets. I loved it when my turn came to carry the flag. Nobody argued the morality of wars back then. It was a simpler and more innocent time.

These days, few of us know anyone in uniform. There will never be another time when every third or fourth house in the neighbourhood has a star in the window, and there will never be another war that so profoundly shapes a generation. There are fewer women like my mother, with both a father and a husband who were soldiers. Soon there will be fewer people like me, who grew up entranced by the deep, mysterious scar on my grandfather's calf. For most families, the times of war and soldiering will pass from living memory.

That is undeniably a good thing. But it's also, in its way, a loss.

———————

Not long ago, my husband got an e-mail from his uncle's wife. Uncle Jack, she told us matter-of-factly, had decided to starve himself to death.

At first we were horrified. But then we agreed that nothing could be more typical of Uncle Jack. A distinguished doctor, he was on intimate terms with mortality, and he was not sentimental about it. He was eighty-five. His health was beginning to fail, and he dreaded disability even more than death. He'd often told us how he'd gently helped more than one suffering patient over to the other side. Now he intended to extend the same mercy to himself. The only difficulty was finding someone to prescribe him the required amount of morphine to ease his discomfort in his final days.

Sure enough, Uncle Jack exited this world ten days after he stopped eating. He left precise instructions for his memorial service, including a list of his favourite hymns and a request for everyone to toast his ashes with large glasses of gin. If only more of us had the cool clear-sighted cussedness of Uncle Jack, this dying business would be a lot less muddled. Yet I'm not surprised we're so irrational about it. Like everybody else, I desire death with dignity. I also desire to live as long as possible, preferably forever.

Today it's easy to reach mid-life without having any close experience of death. The death of a child, once common, is mercifully rare. Our parents may not die until we reach our sixties. On top of that, our culture barrages us with messages that promise we won't get older, just better. For us, retirement is no longer the anteroom of death. It's the beginning of a sort of second childhood where happy, healthy, sexy people frolic in their gated golf communities and cycle through the south of France. Or so the marketers would have us believe.

My husband and I never talk about what we'll do when we get old and feeble. "Honey, just pull the plug," we tell each other, and imagine that we've resolved the matter. Perhaps we'll be as brave and wise as Uncle Jack. But I doubt it.

Not long after Uncle Jack died, it was my father's turn. My dad was a big man, or so he seemed to me. He was broad-shouldered and barrel-chested, with a booming laugh you could hear a block away. He had a big temper, too. When he got mad, you didn't want to be around. He didn't yell. He bellowed.

I always knew my father was a powerful person. My first memory of him dates from a few months after I turned three. It was Easter, and I had on my patent-leather Mary Janes. Daddy took me to the construction site where our new house was being built—a tiny 1950s bungalow that seemed very grand to me. There were piles of lumber and mounds of earth. The house was partly framed up, and together we walked through the spaces where the rooms would be. My shiny Mary Janes got caked with mud, and I was mortified. But I was proud too—proud that my dad was the boss of the construction site, and could make such a big important thing happen. These memories come back to me in bits and pieces, at times when I least expect them.

Half the people I know seem to be burying their fathers about now. We're in our fifties, and the dads are in their eighties, and the actuarial tables don't lie. For most of us, it's our first experience of death in the nuclear family—the loss of someone with whom we share half our genes, someone who's known us since the day we were born. It's a sobering rite of passage. Better get on with things, because now it's you who's on the front lines of mortality. You count the years between your age and your dad's: twenty-four. Scarcely an eye blink.

I wonder if we Boomers stay in denial about mortality because our parents live so long. So long as they're alive, you can still think of yourself as someone's kid—even as you grow wrinkled and arthritic. So long as they're alive, there's someone to say, "I'm proud of you" or "You did good, kid." Your parents (and their parents) were the only people you could count on for unconditional love. And where will you find that, once they're gone?

Parental approval is a potent force, no matter what age you are, and even if you aren't particularly close. Until he lost interest in his computer, my dad subscribed to *The Globe and Mail* online just so that he could read my column. I was ridiculously pleased with that.

When I was younger, my dad's real life was sailing. He was good at it. All my parents' friends were sailors, and their social life revolved around the harbour, which my dad ran for fifty years. I knew he was the most important person at the harbour because he was in charge of the money in the Coke machines. Every so often he'd bring home heavy bags of dimes, nickels and quarters for us to sort out and seal into coin rolls and count up before he took the money to the bank. I was proud to be entrusted with such a big responsibility.

Later on, of course, I came to realize that my father wasn't really so powerful after all. No father is. His marriage to my mother failed. So did his business. He remarried and had two more daughters, and then he had a heart attack that changed his life. His own father had died of a heart attack at forty-nine. After that, Dad had more bypasses and stents and angioplasties than anyone could count. He was lucky to live as long as he did. The miracles of modern medicine extended his life by thirty years.

For a time after my parents split up, I thought my dad and I didn't have anything in common. But I only had to look in the mirror to know that wasn't true. He gave me my droopy eyelids and my red nose, my high blood pressure and my taste for silly jokes and swearing. He gave me my love of newspapers, and language, and word play. He gave me my three sisters and my brother, and, when I was small, the feeling that I was loved and special. That feeling is a powerful and important thing.

Daddy mellowed out as he got older, the way men tend to do. We didn't see each other very much. He and his wife moved down south to a place that was a day's travel away. He took to writing me short but pungent e-mails about his thoughts on politics. "Bush is an asshole," he would write, long before that judgment became conventional wisdom. Dad always was a liberal, which made him an outlier in the heavily Republican enclave where I grew up. It was one of his best features.

In the last year of his life, my father lost interest in most things, just as my father-in-law had done before his death. He turned inward and became quieter. He stopped reading the paper, stopped sending me cranky e-mails, stopped eating. His bellow became a raspy whisper, and he became frail and small. His death was a tremendous shock, as the death of a parent always is, but it was hardly a surprise. It's the one common catastrophe.

Chapter Fifteen

Coming Home

The summer of 1967 was a watershed in my life. I had finished high school in Toronto and was about to go off to university. I was impatient for freedom and adulthood. I was thrilled to be rid of my hateful girls' school uniform, and especially of my clunky black oxfords. They were the very antithesis of fashion back then. Not coincidentally perhaps, they had the same deterrent effect on potential romance as a medieval chastity belt.

Somewhere out there was the Zeitgeist, and I yearned to join it. In San Francisco, a bunch of hippie groups had united to declare a Council for the Summer of Love. The *San Francisco Chronicle* described them as "the good hippies," defined as the ones who "wear quaint and enchanting costumes, hold peaceful rock 'n' roll concerts, and draw pretty pictures (legally) on the sidewalk, their eyes aglow all the time with the poetry of love." The season's signature lyrics were all about going to San Francisco and wearing flowers in your hair.

My girlfriends and I had no way to get to San Francisco. But we did get to Expo, which was almost as good. My friend Susan's dad's company had rented a luxury apartment in Montreal for the summer, and he agreed to let us use it for an entire blissful week. It was the first time any of us had been allowed to travel so far from home on our own, free of the watchful eye of adults.

Expo was spectacular. For one brief moment—never equalled before or since—Canada was where it was at. The world had declared that we were cosmopolitan and hip. The Jefferson Airplane came to play—for free—at Place Ville Marie, and Grace Slick sang "White Rabbit." What better validation of our hipness could there be? The nation was about to leave behind the dull old guys (Lester Pearson, Paul Martin Sr.) and embrace the hip, irreverent and phenomenally seductive new guy (Pierre Trudeau).

My friends and I were dazzled by the Czech Pavilion and Moshe Safdie's Habitat. But the real intoxication was being free, and on our own. Naturally, we did certain things that would have horrified our parents, had they known. We bought an entire bottle of wine, and drank it. We even may have smoked a joint. Best of all, we invited boys to come and stay with us. Susan invited her forbidden boyfriend, a dark, exotic European. Her father had caught them together, and chased the boyfriend down their leafy, old-Toronto street with a shotgun.

Susan was the only girl I knew who may not have been a virgin, and I envied her audacity and her carnal knowledge. I invited a boy named Jack, a romantic, sweet-natured redhead who seemed to be madly in love with me. I was filled with equal parts of hope and fear that something dangerously illicit might happen.

Those were the days when you were still supposed to be a virgin, and if you weren't, you kept quiet about it. But the Summer of

Love was changing all of that forever. In San Francisco, ordinary girls just like me, with flowers in their hair, were making sweet, innocent, guiltless, blissed-out love with shaggy gentle boys who tried their best to look like John Lennon. They were rejecting the uptight hypocrisy of their parents' generation and creating a more honest and authentic way to live (or so they thought). Timothy Leary was urging them to turn on, tune in, drop out. The emerging culture was infused with a new spiritual energy. People really did believe that peace, love and understanding would change the world.

Today, all my friends recall that summer as a magical time, in some ways the best they ever knew. My future husband, who was then nineteen, spent the summer working at Expo, living on his own in Montreal, and trying to persuade girls to have sex with him. The world was full of possibility. We were educated, affluent and hopeful. We didn't think how lucky we were to be reaping the bonanza of post-war prosperity created by our parents, while at the same time categorically rejecting everything they stood for.

To today's seventeen-year-olds, 1967 is as remote as 1927 was to us when we were seventeen. The generation that came of age between 1927 (the year my mother was born) and 1967 endured a depression and a world war and stifling social rigidity. That world seems as dead and gone as the Victorian age. But in some ways, 1967 is still with us. Even though the Summer of Love generation was ridiculously wrong about almost everything, the cultural upheaval we unleashed has reshaped our world. Equal rights for blacks, women and sexual minorities are all part of that. Our values, tastes and cultural preferences are far closer to our children's than our parents' were to ours.

Jack and I never did make love. We were too timid, I guess. He was a sweet boy, so I was sad about that. I was about to head off to an American university that was becoming a hotbed of progressive radicalism, and I was convinced I'd be the only virgin in the entire freshman class.

I don't know where Jack is today. Sometime in mid-life, he became deeply religious and reverted to the old-world spelling of his name. Somewhere I still have the volume of poetry he wrote for me, in an album of fine paper bound in leather. Susan's exotic boyfriend died in an accident a few years later. She married someone else, and had four kids. The summer after Expo, my future husband drove to San Francisco with some buddies. On the way back they were stopped by the U.S. Border Patrol, which discovered a stray pot seed in somebody's suitcase. He spent the next three weeks in the Erie County jail, where his bail was set at $100,000.

A few weeks after my trip to Expo, I started university. To my amazement, almost everyone in my class was still a virgin.

The Summer of Love was the best of times. The world would never seem so fresh, so new, so full of cultural optimism again. After that came assassinations, race riots and a bitterly divisive war. In 1971 I moved back to Canada because the United States had become a scary place. But for one giddy summer, at least, we believed John Lennon, who sang that all you need is love.

———

More than four decades later, I still think Canada is where it's at. I'm hugely proud of the United States for electing Barack Obama. But in some ways America is still a scary place. You can always tell when you've crossed the border into the U.S. Even little airports have at least one heavily armed man in combat uniform, ready to protect the homeland. Those big weapons, prominently displayed, give me a jolt. Military might is one of the ways America defines itself.

Not long ago, I flew down to North Carolina to spend a few days with the American half of my family. It is not like any place in Canada at all, except perhaps Alberta. The right to bear arms is big there. Everywhere you go there are fireworks for sale, along with great southern barbecue. The supermarkets are stocked with aisles and aisles of fabulous, cheap California wine.

"Don't put magazines in your suitcase if you don't want it opened," warned my American sister, Carrie. She works for Homeland Security at O'Hare International Airport in Chicago, searching checked luggage that looks suspicious. On the X-ray machines, she explains, innocent magazines look like plastic explosives that have melted slightly at the edges. She has searched thousands of bags. She's found an amazing array of sex toys, but never any explosives.

My other American sister, Carol, is busy raising four young kids and doesn't have much time to worry about terrorists. She's more concerned about the terrible economy. She worries about bad influences on TV, and tries to make sure her kids watch programs that have a moral point. She recently joined a local Baptist church, and has been born again.

Because I'm a Canadian of American descent, travelling in the United States always reminds me of my mixed identity. And like most people whose lives have straddled the border, my feelings about my two countries are also mixed. There are many things I admire about the United States. Despite its crimes and sins, I still think it is the greatest force for good the world has ever known. There's also plenty about Canada that drives me nuts, starting with our national sanctimony complex. Clifford Krauss, a former Toronto bureau chief for *The New York Times,* is dead-on when he describes Canada as a dictatorship of virtue.

And yet, I've never felt luckier to live here.

In the United States once the housing bubble burst, everything collapsed at once—house prices, home sales, car sales, jobs. Cities and school districts across the country are running out of money because their pension funds invested in zombie assets and their credit is no good. Florida and California are flat broke. This couldn't happen in Canada, since we all share our wealth with one another. Each part of Canada is convinced that it's getting screwed by all the other parts—but maybe it's this sense of mutual grievance that holds us together.

In Canada we had only a few sub-prime mortgages. Our banks don't need to be bailed out. Who ever knew that poky, conservative Canada would turn out to be such a pillar of financial rectitude amidst the smoking ruins? Who would have guessed that Canada's boring old banks would be the model for the new world financial system?

In the U.S., California has joined forty other states that have passed laws banning same-sex marriage. It is now legal in five states, but in Virginia, where some of my relatives live, same-sex partners are barred from basic pension rights and can't even help make medical decisions for their loved ones. Here, in Canada, they can get married. This story made headlines around the world, and the fact of it still astonishes me. It makes me proud for us. And even though some people are troubled by same-sex marriage and others are bitterly opposed, it's worth remembering that gay couples in Canada have achieved a legal and moral status found in only a few places south of the border.

In the U.S., more than twenty states are looking for ways to sneak creationism back into the curriculum. In Canada, radical educators are looking for ways to sneak phonics back into the curriculum.

In the U.S., the abortion wars rage on (even though the chances of *Roe v. Wade* being overturned are now slimmer). In Canada, Henry Morgentaler was given the Order of Canada.

The U.S. is piling up future pensions it can't possibly meet and wrestling with reforming its expensive, inefficient health-care system. Canada has the best-financed public pension plan in the world and our health-care system, with all its flaws, is miles ahead of theirs.

The U.S. has a growing oil-supply problem. We're up to our wazoo in oil—even if some of it is considered "dirty."

The Obama administration is rebuilding bridges burned during the Bush years but the U.S. is still the most hated and feared country in the world. When you're the world's only superpower, it goes with the territory. Nobody hates Canada because nobody cares about us one way or another. We don't count for much in the world, but that's not necessarily a bad thing. Nations that don't count for much are less likely to need men with weapons guarding every little airport.

Don't bother getting smug about all this. If you feel the urge, just remind yourself about the embarrassment that is Ottawa.

Much of our good fortune came our way by luck, not design, and I often think we're rich despite ourselves. We have the immense good luck to share the continent with the wealthiest, most successful and most benign (yes, benign) empire in the history of the world. We were so inconsequential that they never bothered to try to take us over after 1814. They never even bothered to extract levies for defending us. We're like the obscure junior cousins of a fabulously powerful family. We get to share the wealth, but not the headaches, and they supply the protection. And we get the luxury of griping about how they screw things up. What could be better?

Americans are like family to me—our lives are inextricably entwined in complicated ways. I love them, and sometimes they drive me nuts. They're wonderful to visit, but I wouldn't want to live with them anymore.

When I flew back to Toronto from the United States, I was careful not to pack my magazines. When I arrived, there were no men with guns. The signs above the Customs officials said, WELCOME TO CANADA/BIENVENUE AU CANADA.

I was happy to be home.